. . . from Margaret Jensen's latest book,
PROP UP THE LEANIN' SIDE . . .

Without a prop, the farmer can do nothing for the leanin' side of his old barn. The wind and rain will wear against the sagging wood, in time causing total collapse. But the wise farmer is sensitive to the first signs of stress. He watches carefully because his barn is very important to him. He will be there at just the right time with a strong supportive prop. With the right support he can make the barn stand as good as new.

I remember a prayer I heard a long time ago, "Oh, Lord, please prop up my leanin' side." And I think, *We all have "leanin' sides" that need some "proppin' up."*

**Other HERE'S LIFE PUBLISHERS books
by Margaret Jensen:**

Stories By the Sea
A Nail In a Sure Place
Violets for Mister B
Papa's Place
Lena
First We Have Coffee

Margaret Jensen

Prop Up the Leanin' Side

Here's Life Publishers

Third Printing, March 1992

Published by
HERE'S LIFE PUBLISHERS, INC.
P. O. Box 1576
San Bernardino, CA 92402

Cover design by Cornerstone Graphics
Interior design by Jean Bryant

Library of Congress Cataloging-in-Publication Data
Jensen, Margaret T. (Margaret Tweten), 1916-
    Prop up the leanin' side / Margaret Jensen.
            p.   cm.
    ISBN 0-89840-335-9
    1. Meditations. 2. Jensen, Margaret T. (Margaret Tweten), 1916- .
I. Title. II. Title: Prop up the leaning side.
BV4832.2.J463   1992
242—dc20   91-39307
                                CIP

Scripture quotations are from *The New American Standard Bible,* © The Lockman Foundation 1960, 1962, 1963, 1968, 1971, 1972, 1975, 1977.

For More Information, Write:
L.I.F.E.—P.O. Box A399, Sydney South 2000, Australia
Campus Crusade for Christ of Canada—Box 300, Vancouver, B.C., V6C 2X3, Canada
Campus Crusade for Christ—Pearl Assurance House, 4 Temple Row, Birmingham, B2 5HG, England
Lay Institute for Evangelism—P.O. Box 8786, Auckland 3, New Zealand
Campus Crusade for Christ—P.O. Box 240, Raffles City Post Office, Singapore 9117
Great Commission Movement of Nigeria—P.O. Box 500, Jos, Plateau State Nigeria, West Africa
Campus Crusade for Christ International—100 Sunport Lane, Orlando, FL 32809, U.S.A.

Dedicated to

Dr. Robert Judson Carlberg

who has spent a lifetime
"proppin' up leanin' sides."

Not only as a son and a brother, but also as a husband to our daughter Janice and as a father to Heather and Chad, Jud has always been there to prop up the leanin' sides so each one could realize the godly potential in his or her life.

It was Jud the son-in-law who brought me to my first writers' conference at Gordon College, where I met Les Stobbe, who in turn propped me up to write *First We Have Coffee*.

It was Jud the husband who encouraged our daughter to stretch her wings and fly in her creative gifts.

Proppin'-up people don't usually make headlines; they are too busy making others look good.

Behind the scenes, on various boards, Jud's quiet listening ear and heart make diplomacy work. If there's a choice, he opts for mercy versus law.

After many years as Dean of the Faculty at Gordon College, Jud was given a beautiful award:

*The Council of Independent Colleges
1990 Dean's Award
For exemplary contributions
to the Academic Deanship
presented to R. Judson Carlberg*

For many years of work with C.I.C.'s chief academic officers, you have given selflessly of your time, expertise, and wisdom to enhance the profession as a whole.

The mark of your leadership is evident in the work of deans nationwide for whom you have been a mentor and friend.

Through this award your colleagues recognize and thank you for your instruction, your dedication and your inspiration.

OCTOBER 1990

P. S. I have an idea God would sum it up in His award:

"Well done, good and faithful servant,
for proppin' up the leanin' sides of my people."

CONTENTS

ACKNOWLEDGMENTS

A special thank you to my family, especially Harold, my husband, who still believes that Grandma can tell stories.

Thank you to my Here's Life Family who turns my stories into books.

Thank you, Les Stobbe, Dan Benson and Jean Bryant.

All these wonderful people know how to "prop up my leanin' side."

After this book was written, my world was suddenly changed.

On the morning of October 31, 1991, within moments, my Harold, who was my strongest prop, was suddenly taken from my arms and into the arms of his loving Savior.

The family of God came immediately to prop up our family, and we are waiting for the great reunion when we are all Home.

In the meantime, as for me and my house, we will continue to serve the Lord.

Thank you, Harold.

The publisher lovingly dedicates this book to the memory of Harold Jensen, the author's beloved husband, who went to be with the Lord Jesus Christ on October 31, 1991, and is enjoying eternity with his Savior.

Harold, we miss you . . . and Margaret, we love you.

by encouraging words . . .

---

1 "You V.I.P. and Don't Know It!"

THE SMALL CLOCK beside our bed sounded its alarm, too big a noise for a pretty brass clock. It was 4:30 A.M. My husband rolled out of his side of the bed and I sleepily headed for the coffeepot.

Why do we always have to catch the 6:30 flight to Chicago? I asked myself. Then the coffee began perking cheerfully and the day looked brighter. After all, my good-natured husband took it all in stride, humming along with the sound of the electric razor as it blended into the sounds of the morning.

After a quick cup of coffee, a verse for the day and a prayer for safety, we got the bags into the car and

11

were off toward the Wilmington New Hanover County International Airport. The streets were dark and deserted—even the dawn didn't want to get up at that hour. Before long, though, it reluctantly slipped around the edge of town awakening the sleepy inhabitants.

The Charlotte airport teemed with passengers. The walk to B terminal was long, and my bag was heavy. *Next time I won't take so many books along,* I thought. But then, I said that last time. A hug and a prayer, and I climbed the steps to the waiting plane while Harold stood waving in the early light. I was on my way to Chicago, my town for many previous years. There I would change planes and go on to a convention in California.

Waiting for my late flight in the Chicago airport, I settled down with an open book in my lap. A young black girl sat down next to me and began rustling the pages of a magazine. I looked at her over my book.

"Oh, I see you are reading a Christian magazine, a very good one," I offered.

"I know." She kept reading.

I turned back to my book. Curiosity got the best of me; besides, I should always be ready to witness about God's love. "Are you a Christian?"

"Yes, ma'am."

"Oh, that's wonderful. So am I."

"I know."

Back to my book. I wasn't getting too far in this conversation, but I wanted to know more. "Where are you from?" I asked.

"I'm country, just got a box number," she replied.

I went back to my book again. Usually I am very happy to be in my book and I don't begin conversations, but this young woman intrigued me.

"Where are you going?" I persisted.

"California."

"Oh, isn't that exciting! So am I."

"I know."

Back to my book.

Mary laughed so hard
she doubled up on the bed.

Then she gently touched my arm and spilled out her humble story.

"I'm so scared—I never traveled before. But my husband is a country preacher and he said, 'You go to the convention and learn something.' We are just country people, only have a box number. I'm scared to go the convention alone. Maybe I won't get the right plane. 'Just ask,' my husband said. 'We can't tell how God works, so just go.'

"I was so scared," she confessed. "I prayed, 'Please, God, let me meet someone I know.' Then I saw you! See, you are the speaker! Here is your picture!" She opened the brochure. "You V.I.P. and I followed you all over the airport and sat beside you because I know you. Besides that plane won't go down, no way, when you're the speaker."

I closed my book. I felt a lump in my throat.

"When we get to California someone will pick you up in a fancy limousine; you V.I.P., and if I stick close to you, will you tell them I'm with you? Then I get to ride in the limousine with you."

We laughed together out of pure joy, and I told her, (Mary, she said her name was) to stick with me. We would go to the convention together.

Sure enough, a limousine came and Mary stuck like glue. After finding the registration desk, we went our separate ways with a promise to meet later.

The bellhop led me to my lovely room. He also showed me an adjoining room with a magnificent view of mountains and palm trees. By the flowers and the basket of fruit on the table, I realized it was prepared for a special guest. So as we left I closed the door adjoining the rooms. Then it was time to unpack my clothes and iron them, shower, and stretch out for a short nap before the evening banquet.

The convention was great—a thousand happy, talkative women, and a number of great speakers. My beautiful Mary managed to find me even in that crowd. She was my shadow. Then it was time to leave, and while I was packing I heard a knock at my door. It was my Mary.

"Oh," I said to her, "I forgot to show you the room with the view." Turning the knob, I was surprised when the door opened. "I don't know who was supposed to come here, but believe me, it must have been

an important person. Look, Mary, flowers and fruit—
and no one showed up."

Mary curiously peeked at the card in the flowers,
and burst into joyous giggles. "This room was for you!
These flowers and fruit are for you!"

"What? A two-room suite for me?"

Mary laughed so hard she doubled up on the
bed. Pointing her finger at me she finally managed to
say, "You V.I.P. and don't know it!"

I gave her the flowers and fruit. She looked like
a happy bride walking down the hall, chuckling, "You
V.I.P. and don't know it."

On the heels of her joyous laughter I seemed to
sense, deep within my soul, a loving Father with out-
stretched arms saying, "Oh, My children, you V.I.P. and
don't know it. I have baskets of blessings for you and
you don't even read the card. You close the door to My
promises."

I could almost hear the country preacher's admonition, "Go to the convention and learn something."

I learned something: Read the card. The promises are for us.

Thank you, my lovely friend Mary, for your
encouraging words.

TO ENCOURAGE

Think of an encouraging word to share with a V.I.P. in your life today.

> How delightful is a timely word!
> (Proverbs 15:23)

> Therefore encourage one another, and build up one another (1 Thessalonians 5:11).

The chapters that follow share the stories of some special people who encourage others in unique ways.

by supportive companionship . . .

---

2 The Family Memory Album

LIKE A FAMILY ALBUM, my memory stores pictures of people across the pages of my years. Turning the pages, I remember strong and gentle people who need other people.

Framed in my mind is the chicken farmer in his bib overalls, tall and gaunt, standing by his wife's hospital bed when she was my patient so long ago. Through the years she had helped him raise twelve children, worked the farm with him, and shared his successes and failures. Now she had walked through the valley of the shadow of death and back into the land of the living.

She had told me about her husband, "He just walks soft-like through life."

He would quietly steal into her hospital room and stand there, twisting his bent-up hat in his hands. Once he said, "Ain't no way I can raise chickens without my woman." There were tears in his eyes and I heard him whisper softly, "Oh, Lord, how I need her."

I knew what he meant and so did his faithful wife. He really was saying, "You are a V.I.P., and I love you." She was his support. She understood him. She understood the strange language of love. It wasn't the work but her supportive companionship that made the difference. She was always there for him.

I understand that, too, because Harold, my husband, is always there for me. It still makes me smile to remember a picture of myself and Harold proudly showing off yet another remodeling project to our daughter Jan.

It all began when Harold saw the yellow pad with the list:

1. a new image for the old bathroom
2. paint
3. paper
4. shutters
5. curtains
6. new chest

"Oh, no, here we go again," he said. Then he called to me, "Don't you ever run out of projects?"

I reminded him that *his* daughter Jan (*our* daughter Jan) gave me the idea to make lists. And she is so much like him. "Why, Harold, she looks like you, and she is meticulous and organized—and so creative—just like you!" I could tell he was weakening.

But he responded, "Now, Margaret, Larry built a new bathroom for you, so don't worry about the old one. I couldn't care less! Besides we really need a new tub. This one has a rust spot."

I added number 7 to the list:

7. a new rubber mat to cover the rust spot.

> I knew I was getting somewhere when
> he ordered a strawberry sundae
> and laughed with the waitress.

"Let's go to Swenson's for lunch," Harold chirped cheerfully.

I knew he was trying to distract me, but I responded, "Great! Then we can look at wallpaper across the street."

We went to Swenson's and over an egg salad sandwich and good coffee we talked about the bathroom.

"You have done such a good job, painting and papering everything and no one does it quite like you, Harold." It was working. "I think your bathroom should have a new look. After all you are the V.I.P. in this house. You work so hard to landscape and plant. You deserve a nice bathroom."

I knew I was getting somewhere when he ordered a strawberry sundae and laughed with the waitress. Then he brought up the problem of the old tub. "We should spend the money on a new tub."

"Forget the tub," I countered. "I'll put a new mat over the rust spot. Besides, you shower. I'll close the shower doors and the drab tile won't be noticed."

Another cup of coffee, and I ordered buttered pecan ice cream with hot caramel sauce. This was work and I needed all the energy I could get. I looked out the window at the wallpaper store and approached the subject again.

"You always said that wallpaper brightens up a room. I thought that if we picked out some really spectacular paper, no one would notice that dull plastic tile."

He was listening.

And so we checked out the wallpaper and, sure enough, found the most beautiful Williamsburg blue stripes with delicate pink flowers.

Harold carried the paper to the car and began to join in the spirit of the project. "Well, we might as well go to Lowes and get the shutters."

Happily I agreed and almost skipped down the aisle toward the shutters. Projects are such fun!

We bought paint to match the white in the wallpaper, and he found just the chest that would fit in an awkward corner.

Then the project began in earnest. While Harold painted, I sewed organdy curtains to go above the shutters. When the papering was done we covered the linoleum floor with a soft carpet. In the corner sat the newly painted chest, a perfect fit. We added fancy soaps and washcloths matching the colors of the wallpaper. They were the crowning touch. Standing back we looked at the transformed bathroom and said, "Wow! Won't Jan be surprised?"

She was!

Jan and her family arrived for their summer vacation, and everyone was given the grand tour of the bathroom. Even the tub looked great with its new mat— and no rust spot visible.

"Oh, Mom, that old bathroom was an eyesore. I can't believe what Dad did. What a difference!"

Yes, we brightened up the old bathroom and along the way we cheered each other up. It was the working together, the supportive companionship, that made the difference. I remembered a prayer I heard a long time ago, "Oh, Lord, please prop up my leanin' side." And I thought, *We all have "leanin' sides" that need some "proppin' up."*

Another picture album, our entire family enduring the hard bleachers at the cheerleading competition, came to mind. We were there to support 12-year-old Sarah. But first, the "pee-wees" went through their paces and the audience roared with laughter, cheers and applause. One tiny cheerleader, facing the crowd and probably looking for her family, suddenly realized she was all alone on the gym floor. She streaked to catch up with her team and the crowd cheered her on.

Then the competition began in earnest. Sarah looked for her family and smiled. Her best friend Becca saw her family and smiled too; then they both became dead serious. Their team's red and white uniforms and pompons seemed to blend as one unit as they kicked, clapped, shouted cheers in unison, twirled and did their acrobatics. We all yelled and clapped for each team, amazed at their discipline and dedication.

I watched her two big brothers (who had had other ideas for a Saturday) sit on the front row to cheer their sister. Ralph, her Dad, left his shop to be there. I left my desk. This was Sarah's day. She was a V.I.P., and we were all there to let her know it.

Sarah's team was number one in her age group. We cheered as our granddaughter received her trophy and a red rose. Pictures, congratulations and hugs—and then we all went home for lunch.

Similar pictures appear again and again in my memory album. This will be Shawn's last year to play high school basketball. We'll be there to cheer. Then comes Eric. We've watched with Jan and Jud while Heather played soccer and we've cheered Chad in soccer games and school plays. We've watched Kathryn play ball and do her acrobatics. In a few short years it will be all over. The games, the plays, the cheerleading, the competition, and all too soon they will be in faraway places where we can't see them in the game of life.

How we need to remind them that they are surrounded by a cloud of witnesses cheering them on. Supportive companionship makes a difference. Our presence is the silent signal that says to another person: "You are a Very Important Person to me."

God wants us to send this same message from Him to all people. He sent His only Son, Jesus, to be with us; He sent the Holy Spirit to be with us; His message is clear: "I love you. You are a Very Important Person to Me."

I am reminded of the line from a song, "Without Him I could do nothing," and the Scripture verse, "With Him, I can do all things" (Philippians 4:13).

Without a prop, the farmer can do nothing for the leanin' side of his old barn. The wind and rain will wear against the sagging wood, in time causing total collapse. But the wise farmer is sensitive to the first signs of stress. He watches carefully because his barn is very important to him. He will be there at just the right time with a strong supportive prop. With the right support he can make the barn stand as good as new.

TO SUPPORT

Are you willing to send the silent signal to someone today? Will you take the time to say "you are very important to me" by supporting him or her with your presence? God sends this message to us. He promised:

> My presence shall go with you, and I will
> give you rest (Exodus 33:14).

3 His Eye Is on the Sparrow

WE WERE OUT in the yard. The zinnias filled the flower beds with brilliant colors, and butterflies and bees winged their way over the gardens. Suddenly 15-year-old Eric, our son Ralph's number two son, called, "Grammy, this birdbath needs a good scrubbing. It looks gross." (I've learned this is a favorite word for anything unpleasant.) So Eric decided to tackle both birdbaths with rubber gloves, a bucket of suds and some bleach.

Overhead, the mockingbirds cried out in protest. We were too close to the woods where their young nestled in the branches. But Eric continued to scrub and

24

hose down the birdbaths until they gleamed in the sunshine.

Even after he finished, the mockingbirds continued to protest but he drowned them out with the roar of the mower. When he finished clipping and mowing the lawn, he showered and donned Papa's T-shirt.

"No wonder I can't find my T-shirts," moaned Papa. "The boys put them on after yard work and the girls sleep in them when they spend the night."

No one paid any attention.

"He really doesn't care," was 9-year-old Kathryn's wise observation. "Papa has a drawer full of new ones. I know! He hid the Tootsie Rolls under them." That settled the T-shirt mystery.

Eric and I settled in the "nook," 12-year-old Sarah's term for the breakfast room, and watched the birds through the bay window. Between the two of us, the grilled cheese sandwiches, chips and pickles quickly disappeared.

"Look, Grammy, the birds are afraid of the clean birdbath," Eric observed.

The mama mockingbird flew around the shining birdbath. She probably liked the "gross" look better— she was used to it. A bluejay overhead flew away in apparent disgust. Then a pair of robins came close—and looked puzzled. They always showered together. High in the tree branches the birds complained to each other while the birdbath beamed forlornly in the sun. A pair of doves watched from the roof overhang and decided to sit this one out.

Then a brave crow swooped across the garden to the rim of the birdbath. That did it! The mama mockingbird, no friend of crows, decided to run him off. She called for help and the relatives came, and the crow retreated in disgrace. Confident in her success, the brave mama jumped into the birdbath and splashed happily in the cool water. The catbirds, finches, doves, thrashers, robins, bluejays and cardinals all waited their turn; the crow didn't come back. There would be another day.

Eric and I enjoyed the living video with our lunch.

Across the miles the calls for help come winging their way.

Later that evening after the birds had once again taken their turns at the bathhouse, we watched a pair of bluebirds come together to enjoy the last splash of the day. Quiet settled in the woods and finally in our household as well.

I decided it was a good time to open my mail. One mother wrote: "My son ran away. I don't know where he is." Another said: "I can hardly write. My husband of thirty years ran off with a young secretary. The children are married and I'm all alone in a beautiful, empty condo, deserted and rejected. I can't find God."

And more letters: "My daughter is pregnant. She's only 15 and I can't believe it . . . " "My son's wife left him. Now I have the children . . . " "I lost my husband and oh, how I miss him. I know he's home with the Lord, and I want to go Home . . . " "I mortgaged my house to get my son out of jail; then I lost the house and my son."

I put down the letters and began to write about the day. I thought of the birds and their nests, their mates and their young. They live within God's divine order. A call for help will bring a rescue team to help when danger gets too close to home.

God's divine order for families has been shattered by man's rebellion against God. Across the miles the calls for help come winging their way . . . "Help me; I'm in the far country. Only got a box number."

I wing back God's message, "You V.I.P. and *I* know it."

I write, "God knows, He cares, He loves you. You are the apple of His eye, graven in His hand. Run to God. Don't run away. Run to your faithful church and friends. Don't hide."

We must believe together, pray together, get back to the cross of Jesus Christ where love flows from Calvary. Just a mustard seed of faith will find God's sustaining hand, His flowing grace and gentle mercies. There is no condemnation in God's love. Don't be afraid. Plunge into the fountain of God's redeeming love.

First, we must establish our relationship with God and allow His unconditional love and forgiveness to flow through us. Then we must go to His Word for guidance, and then reach out with love and understanding to others, each one a V.I.P. in God's sight.

My long day came to an end late in the night. I had been writing in my journal, not so much for others, but as a reminder to me to fix my heart. I could almost hear Ethel Waters singing, "His eye is on the sparrow, and I know He watches me." As I settled into my "nest," the melody continued and the message lifted my heart. It takes so little to prop up the leanin' side.

TO WRITE

The process of writing down our heartfelt feelings helps us to clarify issues and ponder possibilities. Try writing your thoughts today. And . . .

> whatever is true, whatever is honorable,
> whatever is right, whatever is pure,
> whatever is lovely, whatever is of good
> repute, if there is any excellence and if any-
> thing worthy of praise, let your mind
> dwell on these things (Philippians 4:8).

---

4 Points
of Light

Lightning and thunder flashed and roared with a vengeance. Then the power went off. Without warning we were plunged into total darkness. In the most exciting part of the drama the TV stopped, the whirl of the dryer halted, and the hum of the refrigerator was stilled. The sounds of living ceased and our world became strangely quiet.

The children made a dash for the candles. Here and there came a point of light that cast a soft glow in a darkened room.

"Grammy, this is fun! Let's tell ghost stories."

"Let's wash the dishes first," I proposed. The Norwegian in me does come out, so we washed dishes by candlelight. Fortunately, we had finished the evening meal, but we'd have to wait for our cup of coffee.

As we settled into the semi-darkness, Harold recalled the days on the farm when kerosene lamps gave the light. He told of the excitement when the electric power came to the rural area. It was a big occasion when that lonely light bulb hung from the ceiling. When darkness came everyone would hunt for the cord and with relief and awe turn on the light.

As we told stories in the darkness, somehow we all felt vulnerable. With the refrigerator off we wondered about the food in the freezer, and then there were the clothes in the washer just soaking. How long could we survive without power?

Years earlier a devastating ice storm shut off the power for several days. A camp stove kept the coffeepot going, and a cooking pot with enough soup to drown in was always hot. I didn't want to smell a camp stove or see a can of soup for a long time. Even the smoke from the fireplace challenged us to keep dry wood in good supply. During that time we used an ice chest to take care of the perishables and we tackled the freezer later. I turned the freezer rejects into dog food, enough to feed a zoo. Eventually it was over.

There comes a time in every life when the power goes off—not just the electrical power, but the power for living. A strange silence settles in and it is easier to sit in the dark than to light the candle of faith. The tragedies of life—a sudden death, a business disaster, a prolonged

illness, or the most difficult of broken relationships—
suddenly plunge one into darkness. Into this darkness
someone has to come to light a candle. This is not the
time for floodlights. It is a time for a quiet proppin' up
of the leanin' side, for bringing the soft candlelight of
hope.

The little girl who was late for supper understood this.

"Why are you late?" her mother asked.

"Susie broke her doll."

"Oh, so you helped to fix the doll?"

"No, I just sat and cried with her."

> We need proppin'-up people
> who recognize our leanin' side
> and quietly light a candle of hope.

She was like my friend, a white-haired patriarch,
Mr. James Mason. He would sit with you until you
could stand, then stand with you until you could walk,
and walk with you until you could run.

We need proppin'-up people who recognize our
leanin' side and who will quietly light a candle of hope.

We need people like Mary—she recognized who
the flowers and the basket of fruit were meant for, and
she showed me that the blessing was meant for me.
God's promises bring precious light to each of us.

Across the world of darkness countless points of light will stand together when you and I not only read the card for ourselves, but also for one another.

One little candle can bring the light of a lot of desperately needed hope.

TO CARE

Who can you light a candle of hope for today?

Let your light shine before men in such a way that they may see your good works, and glorify your Father who is in heaven (Matthew 5:16).

---

5 Let's Have a Party

Just as we finished a special birthday dinner for Chris, we were interrupted by a cheerful voice on the telephone. It was Jeff. "Happy birthday, Chris. Did anyone bake you a birthday cake?"

"No, Jeff, not really." We had planned to indulge in Chris's favorite fudge pie.

"Well, Chris, I just want you to know that I am baking a special cake for you, so come over and we'll have a birthday party."

Chris put the phone down, amazed. "Can you believe that? Jeff is baking a birthday cake for me!"

We all cleared away the remains of our birthday party in such a hurry that my admonition to "save the ribbons" fell on deaf ears. When everything was settled, Chris and I went to Jeff's party. His one-room apartment was decorated, and a punch bowl, nuts, candy and chips were on the counter.

Jeff was all smiles when he took the spice cake out of the oven and carefully decorated it with "Happy Birthday, Chris." He kept the candle count low.

"What a cozy apartment, Jeff," I observed.

"Thank you, ma'am. I had more than fifty people for a Christmas open-house party. Did we have fun!"

His neat apartment was close to the university and he could ride his bike to work. He was part of the crew who maintained the beautiful grounds. Sometimes I could see the crew from our back yard just across from the campus. If I happened to be in the yard, I would hear a happy voice call, "Hey, Margaret! Glad to see you home. Where are you going to next? I don't forget you and I pray for you every day."

After our exchanged greetings he would be gone, but his promise to pray for me lingered in my heart.

Now it was time for cake. But first Jeff surprised Chris with a lovely plant. "I love parties," he explained. "This is my first party of the new year."

"Oh, Jeff, I can't believe you had a party just for me—and the plant is beautiful," Chris said.

We munched our cake and sipped the punch while Jeff took pictures. Next to parties, Jeff's love is photography. A stack of albums stood on the shelf. "My family," he said proudly.

Album after album had pictures of his church family—the V.I.P.s in his life. Often when coming out of church we would hear Jeff's gentle demand, "Just look here and smile." We did! In every situation Jeff managed to catch "his family"—at church gatherings, special occasions, and most of all, his own parties.

We turned the pages of his albums and saw beautiful Cattie, wearing a silly birthday hat and blowing out candles. His beloved pastor Horace Hilton with his wife Tennie, were caught talking, eating, laughing, always a part of the family. When Horace was asked to give the blessing at one of the parties, he thanked God for Jeff who brought the church family together for happy parties. Jeff propped up our leanin' sides!

I can just imagine Jeff looking around
at his family, and it won't surprise me
at all to hear him say,
"Oh, I just love a party."

We continued to turn the pages and marveled at the grace of God in bringing together such a "family." Then our party was over and one more picture was in the camera: Chris with the cake in one hand, a flowering plant in the other.

It was time to say good-night, and Jeff waved happily as we pulled out of the driveway. Tomorrow would be another day, but tonight was a party.

In all my travels, I have seen many albums, but this was the first time I had seen albums filled with the family of God. From every walk of life they came to the foot of the cross where by the precious blood of Jesus they were made one in Christ, part of God's family. The angels in heaven rejoice when God adds one more to His family album.

"I won't forget, Margaret. I'll pray for you every day."

"I'm counting on it, Jeff. I know you won't forget me or your 'family,' " I replied. *We need your prayers*, I thought. *Yes, not only your prayers, but your happy parties to ease the rocky roads of life.* One of these days, maybe sooner than we think, God's family will be called Home to a great celebration in Heaven. I can just imagine Jeff looking around at his family, and it won't surprise me at all to hear him say, "Oh, I just love a party."

TO CELEBRATE

Birthday celebrations are a way of saying you are a V.I.P. to me; I rejoice that you were born. Why wait for birthdays? Celebrate the "being" of the people in your life on other days, in other ways.

Rejoice with those who rejoice (Romans 12:15).

It's a wonderful way to prop up some leanin' sides.

6 The Sisters Are Coming

My garden clippers kept singing a duet with Rudy's clippers. In the quiet of the morning my young neighbor and I clipped around the cedar trees and I filled a garbage container with prickly vines that had entwined their thorny stems around the tree trunks. The winter freeze apparently had destroyed our palm trees and Harold was sawing off the dead, brown branches.

"Don't cut your palms down," a TV gardener had advised. "There is a possibility of life in the depth of the trunk." We doubted that, but we followed his instructions and trimmed the branches but kept the palm. It turned out he was right.

"Whew, it's hot." Rudy stopped to wipe his face. "What in the world are you doing with those clippers, Miss Margaret?"

"I'll tell you, Rudy, why Harold and I decided to tackle this lawn: My sisters are coming!" We both had a good laugh.

"Nothing like company coming to get things done. My mother-in-law is coming!" said Rudy.

With the visitors in mind, we played our clipper duet while Harold mowed the spacious lawn and trimmed the edges. Then Harold and I inspected the flower beds. Each day I had spent one or two hours in a flower bed, and since I have six of them, I had begun two weeks earlier to be sure the weeds were all gone. My sisters were coming!

In the house I had cleaned one room at a time—woodwork, windows and curtains, and I even coaxed Harold to wash ceiling fans and put up sparkling light fixtures. He had groaned, "I know, I know, your sisters are coming!"

Then the day came! The guest rooms were ready, and my Norwegian tablecloth was on the breakfast table, which was set for coffee. The brownies and cookies were cooling and the bread dough I had set early that morning was . . . falling? Not rising? It was just a lump of dough refusing to budge!

"Oh, no! Five loaves of bread falling! Something must be wrong with the yeast," I moaned. My pride plummeted with the five loaves of hard bread that had to be thrown into the woods for the squirrels, raccoons, rabbits and birds.

Then it was time to go to the airport. "Where are you, Harold?" I called. There he was on his knees in the driveway, not praying, but painting a huge sign on oilcloth. With great fanfare he hung the sign up on the clothesline. In bright blue paint, it read:

THE SISTERS ARE COMING! HELP!

> The warm kitchen, the cocoa and toast
> said what he couldn't say in words:
> "You V.I.P.; button up.
> It's cold outside."

They came! Jeanelle, the youngest, Papa's pianist, from Florida; Joyce Solveig, Papa's songbird from Arkansas; Doris, from Greensboro, who went to Wheaton College on a hundred dollars; and Grace, the secretary, accountant and general manager. In Papa's words, "Ja, ja, there is no one like Grace. She should be secretary to the President."

Believe me, five sisters in noisy reunion in our small airport was news! And everywhere we went people continued to notice the joy of our gathering.

One clerk at the mall laughed and called wistfully, "Have fun!" She added, "I lost my only sister and now there is no one to tell the family jokes to."

Someone else watched us laughing together while Joyce told stories in a Norwegian accent. He came by our lunch table. "Sorry to interrupt," he said, "but I just can't help noticing how much fun you are having."

A clerk in a gift shop said, "You ladies have made my day. Not many people have fun anymore. You can't believe the cross and unhappy people who come into our shop."

We had to pull Joyce away from the humorous card display. She and our daughter Janice and Ralph's wife Chris could spend all day laughing at cards.

"Do you remember . . . ?" someone started. And we all remembered.

Remember how Jeanelle begged Mama to let her take her cod liver oil with a fork?

Harold remembered when Doris wanted to run away with him because Papa was on the warpath.

When Grace was a young child someone invited her to spend the night with her daughter, and she said, "Oh, no! My mother needs me!"

"Remember when I got lost in Humbolt Park when the 17th of May Norwegian celebration was in full swing, with parades and bands?" Joyce asked. "And then a booming voice called out, 'Would Pastor Tweten please claim his lost daughter Joyce Solveig?' I was terrified," she recalled, "not at being lost as much as at how Papa would be furious with me. Then he came and swooped me up in his strong arms and cradled me close to him. I felt so loved and safe. I didn't want to move."

I recalled when Papa shook the stove at 5 A.M., and I curled up close to my sisters Grace and Doris. I knew I had another hour before I had to get up for school.

But Papa called, "Margaret, time to get up!"

The kitchen was warm in our second floor Chicago flat. Papa sat in the rocker reading his Bible. On the table was a cup of hot cocoa and six slices of buttered oven toast. I ate quietly. No one interrupted Papa when he was reading, and he always had a book in his hand.

I said, "Tak for maten" (thanks for the food), and kissed him on the cheek, and he said, "Button up! It's cold outside!"

That was all we said. Through the years how often I've wished I had said more. The warm kitchen, the cocoa and toast said what he couldn't say in words: "You V.I.P.; button up. It's cold outside."

We continued to reminisce as we gathered around the piano to sing old hymns and imitate the Norwegian string band. We could never tell if the band sang in Norwegian or in English.

Whenever we get together we usually recall the days we were with Mama. At the end we watched her spirit soar Homeward to be with Papa, Gordon our brother, and our baby sister Bernice, and we knew that Mama saw her Savior face to face.

A friend, observing our joyful visiting, remarked how special it was to see five sisters so close and enjoying each other. Agreeing that it was special for us, too, Jeanelle said, "We were born sisters, but we chose each other for friends."

When an emergency arises, we start the sisters' telephone alert "to pray." When a special joy comes our way, we call "to rejoice." Each of us is a unique individual, but our mutual love for the Lord, for our families and for each other binds us together as one.

When we were children Mama would say, "Always love each other." And as we grew older she reminded us, "Love each other and stay close in your hearts."

When the years turned our hair grey and the storms of life had left its scars, and Mama knew she was going Home, she looked at us five sisters and said, "What have I ever done to deserve such beautiful daughters?" Then she added, "Always love each other, stay close and take care of each other."

Now we are getting older and through the years we have loved each other, and we stay close in our hearts even when miles separate us. Now is the time to take care of each other.

The days of joy came to an end. Too soon it was time to part. We huddled together as Harold lovingly prayed over the sisters, asking God to keep us all in His loving care. Doris and Grace headed toward Greensboro on Route 421. Jeanelle and Joyce winged their separate ways by plane.

The sign was still hanging there: "THE SISTERS ARE COMING!" I didn't want to take it down.

Our children and grandchildren are still talking about their aunts and the day the sisters came. Harold and I laughed together about the housecleaning (who noticed?), the manicured lawn, trimmed hedges and weedless flower beds—even the five loaves of bread in the woods.

Somehow it really wasn't for anyone to notice. It was just our way of saying, "You V.I.P. and I want you to know it."

It's easy when we prop up the leanin' side from our hearts.

TO PREPARE

By our preparations we show how important people are to us. God has prepared more than we can imagine for those who love Him:

> Things which eye has not seen
> and ear has not heard,
> And which have not entered the
> heart of man,
> All that God has prepared for
> those who love Him (2 Corinthians 2:9).

Make special preparations today for those you love, those who love you. You'll be amazed at how much it props up the leanin' side.

by sensitive response . . .

---

7 Some Ways to Be a Blessing

One day our 11-year-old granddaughter Sarah cried, "Grammy, Kathryn is making fun of my big feet."

"Big feet? Let me look," I said. "Oh, my, you have princess feet, long and narrow, like your cousin Heather and like Princess Diane. Yes, princess feet. That's what you have."

"Well, what kind do I have?" Kathryn, 9 years old, held up her sturdy foot.

"You have queens' feet, good sturdy feet. Yessir, Queen Kathryn."

That did it! I began to call them "Princess Sarah" and "Queen Kathryn." We even watched for sales and one day found a $100 pair of Evan-Picone shrimp-colored shoes on a clearance table for $15. Princess shoes! Sarah was elated. We also found an inexpensive matching sweater. The princess had her day!

Then it was Kathryn's turn. She came bounding into the room one day excitedly calling to Papa to look at her shoes. "See the tag?" she asked. "One-hundred and twenty dollars! Black patent leather with a bow!"

"A hundred and twenty dollars?" Papa slipped into his best horror act.

Kathryn giggled delightedly. "Look, Papa, Mama found these ladies' shoes for $15 on a clearance rack. I'll have them for next Christmas. They're too big for me now, but just right for queens' feet."

A little proppin' up the leanin' side never hurts.

A similar situation occurred one time when a lonely girl in leg braces came to me with tears in her eyes. "I've been invited to a wedding and I hate my braces," she said.

"Oh, honey," I responded, "get someone to make you a long skirt, and wear a pretty blouse. No one will see anything but your beautiful face."

Later I received a picture of a beautiful girl in a long dress. Sometimes it takes so little to prop up the leanin' side!

My mother knew the importance of responding to the circumstances of a child. It happened sixty years ago, but I remember as though it were only yesterday.

The ad in the newspaper read: "Mother's helper, $1 a day." I was elated!

If there was anyone with experience, it would certainly be this 14-year-old preacher's daughter who had helped mother since the age of 2. Five younger sisters and a brother stuck in the middle qualified me for the job. A telephone call confirmed the fact that I was hired. One dollar a day meant six dollars a week. A fortune in depression days!

> Strange that someone so large and strong can't clean the kitchen . . .

I boarded the Diversey Avenue bus and rode to the affluent part of Chicago, close to the lake. The view from the second floor flat was magnificent. I stood in awe of the spacious carpeted rooms and the beautiful furniture. Exquisite lamps and pictures gave the flat an air of elegance and extravagance. The china cabinet was filled with sparkling crystal and beautiful china. I couldn't imagine how anyone could have so much.

Then reality came!

"I want you should first clean the kitchen," instructed the mother. I wondered where the children were. Wasn't I a mother's helper?

Oh, yes, the kitchen. There it was, a sink full of dirty dishes, not only today's, but apparently from two or three days.

I shuddered! Mama had never allowed dishes to stand in the sink. You wash, rinse, dry, put away, scour the sink, sweep the floor and take out the garbage. That's what mama meant by washing dishes.

(I remember going visiting with my mama when I was very young. While the women drank coffee in the parlor I noticed a sink of dishes. Since Norwegian honor was at stake, I pulled up a stool and proceeded to wash them.)

My mistress continued, "When you finish the dishes, clean the stove."

It was filthy!

I knew about cleaning old gas stoves. Mama had us clean and polish the stove every Saturday.

"Oh, yes, the ice box," she added. I knew to empty the water pan underneath and scrub away the mold.

"I have to go shopping, but there are a few things I couldn't send to the laundry, like linen underwear and stockings. You can wash them in the tub and hang them on the back porch."

I watched my new employer reach for her pocketbook and move her large frame toward the door. *Strange that someone so large and strong can't clean the kitchen,* I thought. Her soft hands certainly didn't look like Mama's hands. The diamond rings sparkled on her hand and a gold watch reminded her that she was late.

Mama had one gold band on her finger, no watch. Her strong hands smelled of Fels Naphtha soap and were so gentle when she held us.

"Oh, a sandwich you can fix for lunch. We go out to dinner so no one will be cooking. The children are with my sister. Her maid takes care of them today." (Well, that answered one question.) Then she was gone.

The kitchen! First the kitchen! I must be worth that precious dollar.

Mama was quiet,
but there was a twinkle in her eye.

While the dishes soaked I dismantled the stove. The oven had to be scraped with a knife and S.O.S. Then the dishes—wash, rinse, dry, put away, scour the sink, take out the garbage. While the pots and pans soaked I gathered the garbage that was stacked all around the kitchen and took it down two flights of stairs to the incinerator. Back to the pots and pans. Mama's never looked that black. I scraped and scoured with S.O.S. until my fingers were raw.

Next the floor! How could floors be so sticky? With scrubbing and scraping it finally looked like Mama's kitchen floor.

I was so tired I wanted to cry, but the thought of that dollar bill gave me new energy. Two cheese sandwiches and a glass of milk helped ease my hunger and I was ready to tackle the bathtub of laundry.

What a shame that anyone could leave soiled underwear in a tub. No one saw Mama's underwear. It was discreetly laundered and hung in faraway places. Her corset found a safe spot behind the stove, hidden from view. But the only place to hang clean laundry that day was on the back porch for all the world to see —bloomers blowing in the wind, petticoats and nightgowns. Was there no shame? When the tub was scrubbed I tackled the rest of the bathroom. Finally it was clean!

When the door opened, my buxom mistress came in with boxes from Marshall Fields. Since Mama only went to the Logan Department Store for sales, I didn't know anyone could buy so much, especially from Marshall Fields.

"What a day," she moaned. "I didn't even finish. Now, don't forget to polish the furniture. The children's rooms could stand a little cleaning, too."

It was 6 P.M. and she left to go out to eat. Hungry, and oh, so tired, I knew I had to finish. Then it was 8 P.M. I had worked for twelve long hours.

When my mistress returned she handed me a dollar bill and with a flourish announced, "You won't need to come back tomorrow. My maid will be here from her two-week vacation."

Too proud to cry, I boarded the Diversy Avenue bus for home.

When I stumbled into Mama's kitchen, hungry and weary, I could only cry, "Oh, Mama, I'm so sorry. I thought I had a job for all summer. She never said it was to clean the whole house before the maid returned from a two-week vacation."

Mama quietly prepared some food and wiped my tears. I could tell she was deep in thought.

"Come, Margaret, you and I are going back."

I sat in awe beside Mama on the bus. It cost ten cents in carfare, now thirty cents out of that precious dollar.

With quiet dignity Mama confronted the powerful mistress of the lakefront flat. "I believe you took advantage of a young girl who was hired as a mother's helper. I expect you to give her another dollar and our carfare. Don't ever take advantage of a young girl again."

The large woman seemed to shrink in size while Mama's dignity made her seem ten feet tall. Without a word, the woman handed me the dollar and carfare, and Mama said goodnight.

Once again we were on the bus, going home. Mama was quiet, but there was a twinkle in her eye.

That was the unforgettable day when Mama made me feel I was the most V.I.P. in the world. Mama had responded with sensitive determination. I sat up straight! She had really propped up my leanin' side!

Mama's kitchen was warm and clean, the coffeepot was on, and we sliced her homemade rye bread and cheese. Papa chuckled delightedly!

"Ja, ja, in all the world there is no one like Mama."

I fell asleep secure in the order of things.

Another day, just a short time ago, I was tired and eager to be home, but all was not in order. It is all in the letter I wrote to Jan:

Dearest Jan,

My day began at 4:30 A.M., when Daphne Thompson, my gracious Canadian hostess, put on the coffeepot, and I closed my suitcases. I was heading home.

Daphne eased the car out of the driveway; the cat and dog kept watch from the porch. Rachael, the teenage daughter, skipped school and curled up in the back seat to accompany her "mum" the hundred miles to the Saskatoon airport.

Dawn slipped up across the barren fields, and here and there a light came on in a prairie home. Wheat, flax and barley had been harvested and fields stood ready for fall plowing. The road stretched before us and only an occasional truck came our way.

Then it was time to say goodbye, and I was soaring into the morning sun. I settled into my seat and reached for pen and paper. A day to write!

"Are you a writer?" asked my seat companion.

I put down my pen and turned to acknowledge him. We shared a mutual interest in poetry and books. We shared more: our faith in God and His gift of eternal life, and our appreciation for how creativity comes from Him. I autographed a book for him before we landed in the Minneapolis airport, and our paths separated during the routine customs and baggage checks.

One of my bags was missing, but I was too tired to care. Besides I was going home. Sooner or later the bag would come home too.

A gentle young woman came to me, "My bag is missing. And it's my first flight." A young man took charge and we were separated in the line of customs.

An elderly couple, 85 years of age, from England, missed the shuttle so we waited together, then proceeded to the main terminal. We talked of God's care for us and they left with a book to read on their next plane flight.

I had five hours to wait. My yellow pad and pen came out. This is the day I could check something off my list. I would write!

"Hello." When I looked up, I saw the gentle face of the young woman who had lost her luggage.

"Did you find your luggage?" she asked.

"No, but I'm sure it will go to North Carolina." I replied.

"I need my bag because I am going to the hospital, and I don't know anyone."

I put my yellow legal pad and pen away. "Come, honey, sit down with me."

I learned about a young son, 15 months old, that she left in Alaska, and about a husband who had to care for the child. In those moments, I saw courage in a young mother who was facing crucial surgery in a strange city. She carried her X-rays and records in her hand.

"I'm a Christian," she added, "and I prayed that God would lead me to a Christian."

Her eyes shone with faith. We clung to each other in faith and prayer. I had no more books left; all had been given along the way in planes and airports. Even my Bible was in my suitcase. I reached in my bag for my paperback copy of Oswald Chamber's devotional book to leave with her, promising to mail my books later. When it was time for her flight, a kind attendant drove her to the gate. I could hardly let her go, holding her for a moment to pray for God's love to keep her safe.

"Take good care of my girl," I said.

The attendant smiled and I saw the glory of the Lord in his face. I heard him say, "Faith, that's what it takes! Yes, sir, faith!"

Then they were gone.

Turning to the ticket attendants I saw tears in their eyes. The loss of our bags was no accident. I wiped my eyes.

Well, Jan, I didn't get my writing done, so will manage to get this letter off to you. I won't be home until 11 P.M., a long day, and it's not over yet. Who knows what God has planned for the next trip?

Love,
Mother

P.S. Oh, dear, I didn't get this mailed so will tell you the rest of the story. On the next plane I met a businessman from Minneapolis, and when I told him about my friend, he promised to get his secretary to check on her at the Rochester Clinic. Later, I also told our women's group and they sent cards, notes and prayers winging across the miles.

I called the hospital and received a good report. Also mailed all my books, and believe it or not, some of the hospital personnel were familiar with them and my friend from Alaska got so excited that a "celebrity" (ugh) had prayed with her. It was her turn to be V.I.P.

Anyway, she finally got a correct diagnosis and can be treated in Canada. "The prayers of God's people did it," she said.

Love,
Mother

TO RESPOND

By our response to problems we can choose to discourage and destroy, or to encourage and enlighten. Seek a sensitive response to the conflicts you may face today.

> Let all be harmonious, sympathetic, brotherly, kindhearted, and humble in spirit; not returning evil for evil, or insult for insult, but giving a blessing instead; for you were called for the very purpose that you might inherit a blessing (1 Peter 3:8,9).

8 Home Again

My stiff legs could hardly make it down the steps from the plane. I took a deep breath of Carolina air and hurried to the terminal where Harold waited with a welcome home. It seemed that I had never been on so many roads—mountain roads, town roads, rainy roads, snowy roads—California, Wisconsin and Illinois. I had been traveling for sixteen days, and speaking every one of them. Weariness had seeped into my bones.

"Let's get you home and we'll have a cup of tea and you can tell me your wild west stories," encouraged Harold.

It was good to be in the breakfast nook with time to unwind from travel. When I returned home I went from room to room to enjoy the pictures, the soft lamps, special pieces of furniture made by our son Ralph, and gifts of love from all the family. The grandfather clock, our special 50th anniversary gift from the children sounded out 11 chimes. Beautiful sounds of home!

"You wouldn't believe the mountain roads I traveled, and my heart holds the memory of all those wonderful people. I love them," I told Harold. "Believe me, California is wild, and people drive those mountains like they are playing Russian roulette. Am I glad to be in our town with no six-lane freeways! Tomorrow I just want to get into my baggy jogging suit, the red one with the duck. And I'll enjoy my own cooking, my own meatballs and mashed potatoes."

"Don't forget a pie," reminded Harold. "It's been a long time to eat at K & W. I wish I could go with you more, but there is so much to take care of at home."

Then the stories began.

I was so tired after one of the morning sessions, after the long trip the day before and the time change, and was sure I would have an hour to rest before the next session. Believe me, it was wishful thinking. A voice behind me said, "Margaret, there are so many problems represented here and women are lined up to see you."

Beside a peaceful lake sat two chairs in the warm sun, just made for me. "Oh, Lord," I prayed, "I am so weary, and I am no psychologist; so come, Holy Spirit, I need you." I knew that in our weakness we can be strong in Him. That day I discovered it in a new way.

The mother of a 25-year-old man said he was destroying her marriage. "My husband says that our son has to go to work and move into his own apartment."

So what's the problem? I wanted to say, but I didn't. I waited.

"My poor baby doesn't seem to be able to hold a job, and he can't make it on his own."

> As I was seated beside him, he
> chuckled delightedly
> at my expression of surprise.

This time I didn't stay quiet. "Maybe you would rather let your husband go and you can take care of your baby."

"Oh, no. I love my husband," she insisted.

"Then listen to him. Period."

She did. With the help of the pastor and the family the "poor boy" got moved out. In order to eat and pay rent he got a job. Mama was ordered to stay out of it and not supplement his feedings. Mama and Papa went on a trip, hopefully living happily ever after.

Harold continued to listen loyally to my stories.

It was so good to get home to him, to relax and tell it all. He listened quietly while I rambled on. He knew I had to get it said. He also knew that I waited for his comments. After all, we were in this together, the prayers, the hard work, the schedules. We are a team.

"Life was more simple when we were young," he commented quietly. "We worked together within the framework of the Judeo-Christian values. We were taught to love God, obey the law, honor parents, excel in school. The work ethic brought discipline to the mind and body."

We remembered another trip, one that gave me a couple of lovely surprises.

The plane from North Carolina landed in the windy city of Chicago. It was February and I was heading to a women's conference in Highland, Indiana. In Chicago I was met by the coordinator, Grace Beezie, and then continued the journey by car. But first, through an earlier telephone call to Marjorie Del Rosso at the alumni office, we had arranged to stop for a visit and a cup of coffee at the Norwegian American Hospital in Chicago.

Grace and I passed the old landmarks, turned from Division Street, and parked the car at 1044 N. Francisco Avenue. Almost fifty years had gone since I passed through the doors of my old nurse's training school. I wondered how it had stood the test of time. Through Marjorie, a bridge had been kept open between the past and the present. When my books were published, though I had not met her, she sent notes and flowers of congratulations. Now I would meet her!

She suddenly appeared out of nowhere, a tiny woman behind a walker on wheels. Her bright eyes matched her shining personality and within moments we were trying to keep up with her as we had a grand tour of the hospital.

Hugs, smiles, and laughter greeted us down the halls where Spanish, Norwegian and English seemed to blend into one language of the heart. Paintings, soft carpets, and pastel shades on the walls had transformed the barren whiteness into a symphony of color. The old dormitory was now a cafeteria. The nursing school belonged to the past.

It was Miss Hanna's floor, 4th annex, that held me. The old utility rooms brought back the memories of high metal beds, crank-up back rests, the clatter of bedpans and basins. I could almost see Mr. Zeb on the fire escape.

The old building had been remodeled and new wings added. The sounds of yesterday blended with those of today, sounds of compassion and humor, cleanliness and order, efficiency and comfort. It was all there, the sound of a family working together, different cultures blending into the language of the heart—love. All around me I felt the presence of God in the people within the walls of my old training school.

We followed our guide to a private dining room where to my utmost surprise sat former board members, nurses and new friends. One new friend was the Norwegian consul's wife, Mrs. Ohrstrom. Miss Rosie was gone, but I met a lovely young director of nurses. Jenny Matson, the former administrator was gone, but before me stood a handsome young man, the new administrator.

Seated at the table was Mr. Abrahamson, lifelong board member, the brother of my supervisor, Miss Abrahamson. She had been the keeper of the night watch of so long ago. Mr. "A" sat in a wheelchair beside his lovely wife. He was a large man who had devoted his life in service to others. His heart was as big as life, reaching beyond the confines of his hospital room.

As I was seated beside him, he chuckled delightedly at my expression of surprise when I was ushered in to the special luncheon. With a beautiful smile he gave me a lovely gift, an orchid. But he gave me so much more. That sweet reunion was a wonderful reminder to me of God's faithfulness to all generations.

With a promise to return, I left with a song in my heart, and an orchid in my hand, thanks to Mr. A!

Marjorie Del Rosso continues to reach around the world with her heart of love, her tiny frame moving swiftly down the halls with the walker on wheels. She makes each alumnus feel like a V.I.P. as she draws us together in sweet reunion through cards, letters and gatherings. She knows how to prop up the leanin' side!

The grandfather clock struck midnight. It was time to put aside the stories and go to bed. The suitcases were still on the guest bed. Tomorrow would be another day. Harold locked the doors and put on the night lights. We thanked God for a safe trip and prayed for the children. Then I stretched out on the bed and leaned on his arm, floating off to dreamland.

His loyal listening was like his strong arm, proppin' up my leanin' side.

TO LISTEN

When important people speak, it is said, we listen! Is that true? What about the V.I.P.s in our own lives? Are we too quick to speak our opinions, too quick to become frustrated and to cut off those we love? Concentrate today on paying close attention to a V.I.P. in your life and . . .

> be quick to hear, slow to speak and slow to anger (James 1:19).

9 A Present Help

The laughter and chatter of happy women mingled with the sound of coffee cups at breakfast. Then it was time to go in for the meeting. With notebooks and Bibles in hand, the women moved into the retreat center. Enthusiastic singing rang across the valley and an atmosphere of expectancy filled the air. Yet I noticed one woman whose expressionless face seemed to call out for help.

I decided I must meet her. When break time came, I moved slowly to stand casually beside her. *I must be careful,* I thought.

"Hello. What a beautiful morning," I greeted casually.

A dull, listless stare looked back at me. I didn't know what else to say so I took her in my arms and held her. I wanted to weep. I just said quietly, "God loves you."

She stiffened.

Then slowly, in the same flat voice without emotion she began to speak. "I'm having a nervous breakdown. That's what my doctor told me. I don't know why I'm here. Someone paid for me to come and the doctor said it was a good idea. I'm falling apart."

There was silence for a moment and then she continued, "I have a retarded child who needs much attention, but my husband was good to help me."

Then came the blank stare again, looking off into space.

Oh, God, help her, I cried silently. No one seemed to notice us; they all appeared to be enjoying the coffee break. The curtain was opening on one of life's tragedies, and I wanted the drama to end. I wanted this to be a make-believe play. But it was real!

In a flat voice the woman added, "Now my husband is helpless—he had a stroke. And I am having a nervous breakdown. My doctor said so. Life is too hard for me now."

I felt myself crying on the inside, *It's not fair. It is too much for one woman!*

Then it was time to go. I had to speak in the next session. I told my stories of faith in trials, the humor and tears in my Norwegian immigrant family, and Mama's walk of undaunted faith. The audience cried and laughed with me. But my friend stared straight ahead without expression.

Lunch time came; I sat beside her and we ate quietly. There are times when words can't be heard—the heart hurts too much, and the mind is numb with unanswered questions.

Before we left the table I asked her, "What will happen to your child and husband if you collapse?"

> "I began in Genesis
> to write 'praise Him,'
> and I couldn't stop."

We went into the following session where I continued a theme of how God fastens us as a nail in a sure place. Corrie Ten Boom was fastened in a concentration camp, Chuck Colson in a prison, Joni Eareckson Tada in a wheelchair. In these seemingly impossible situations the glory of the Lord shone through His special nails, tough, and hanging in there, by God's grace.

Then I saw the tears trickling down the cheeks of my fragile friend. I knew God's gentle Holy Spirit was quietly at work. The Comforter had come.

The sessions continued. Before I realized it we had come to the closing prayer. I looked for my friend.

There she was, coming toward me. Her face was alive. Strength seemed to flow from her being.

"That question, the one you asked, has been haunting me for two days. You know, 'What will happen to your family if you collapse?' It kept coming back to me. Then I saw it! I was the nail God fastened for them. He would not fail me now." She squared her shoulders and held her head high, "And I won't fail them!

"I'm going home refreshed in my spirit and body. There will be a way to get help and I've decided to go back to my church."

Then she threw her arms around me and we prayed together, cried and laughed. We knew God would see her through.

Later, as everyone was saying goodbye, a small group of women came to tell me that she used to be in their church. They promised to help her. They had paid her way to come and had been praying for her. I was reminded that God has His angels all around, proppin' up the leanin' side.

My friend was one of the last to leave. She gave me a "V for victory" sign and laughed, "No way I can have a nervous breakdown! I'm the only nail my family has."

Later, when my plane soared over mountains and valleys, I put my head back on a pillow and closed my eyes. "Oh, Lord, thank You. The same comfort You gave my Norwegian mama, she in turn gave her seven children. The same comfort we received we also give to Your children. You are the river of refreshing, the endless flow of love, grace and mercy. Take care of this little lady, Lord; please put Your loving arms around her and wrap her in a blanket of your peace."

In my mind came the memory of another retreat where the wife of an airline pilot was surrounded by prayer. She had suffered deep depression when she discovered that their three teenagers were involved in drugs.

"Why weren't you here?" the frustrated mother complained to her husband.

"Hey, I'm giving you a good living. Can't you keep track of the kids?"

The bitterness mounted.

"My dear, let him go!
I just talked with a dozen gals
who'd love a dull husband."

The church family rallied to the family's support, and prayer and counseling came to the children. Within a year they were back in school and doing well.

But the bitterness remained.

The mother wept most of the time. "What can I do?" she cried in my arms during a woman's retreat.

"Praise," slipped into my heart and out from my mouth. Somehow I always resented a glib answer, but this was different.

"I have an idea," I suggested. "Take your Bible and begin to write down all the 'praise Him' verses you can find. Before you begin, let's thank God for your husband, who is a good provider—and don't forget, he is hurting, too. Thank God that your children received help in time and are doing well in school. Then let's thank God for your new strength, the joy of the Lord."

She went to her room to write.

The next day she stood before the entire retreat group and said, "I began in Genesis to write 'praise Him,' and I couldn't stop. During most of the night I kept writing and I really don't know when it happened, but I started rejoicing and now I can't stop."

The prayer of praise was proppin' up her leanin' sides.

I was home from yet another retreat, and while the coffee perked, I donned my baggy jogging suit, red kerchief, and I was ready for the clearing of the scraggly fall garden.

The empty suitcases rested in the attic and the clothes spun in the washer. In a few days I would be on the road again—to New England, then Toronto, Canada. But today I would dig up all the old zinnia plants and Harold would plow the garden for spring. It was a good day.

Everything looked dry and dead except the periwinkles and mums. They nodded at each other, reluctant to leave and determined to welcome the winter with a smile. Too soon, they also would be gone and only green brushes and pines would resist the winds of winter.

Today was warm, the coffee smelled good, and I had set an extra cup for Chris, Ralph's wife. Sure enough, I soon heard the car in the driveway, and Chris bounced in.

"Just have a minute. Have to run errands for Ralph," she said.

We munched on raisin toast and drank coffee.

"You ought to tell Chris the story you told me," Harold chuckled delightedly. "I'm telling you, Chris, you never heard such counseling in your life. I think Margaret should stick to stories and let the Littauers counsel," Harold chuckled delightedly.

Chris urged me on, so I told the story.

It began at the retreat. I was wondering how I could listen to even one more heartbreak when a beautiful woman came sailing in. I instinctively liked her, with her flashing black eyes, dark curly hair and expressive Italian gestures.

She fairly trembled, announcing, "I have a problem!"

I wanted to laugh, but I didn't. I waited. Harold had told me to do that, wait and be quiet. ("You can't solve every problem, Margaret. Just let them talk and perhaps they can hear their own solution.") I waited and stayed quiet; besides, I was too weary to talk.

"I'm 40," she declared.

"Oh, you do have a problem." I couldn't resist that one. "I'm only 73."

"I was just born again," she continued. "It was a wonderful experience of being made new and knowing what it means to have a right relationship with God."

That didn't sound like a problem, but I was quiet. Harold would have been proud of me.

She went on. "Also, we just started a new business. It's going great! And I have three beautiful children."

I wanted to laugh. She had a problem? So who needs solutions when you have such problems?

"It's my husband!" she blurted. "He is dull, and I mean dull!"

I was beginning to come to life. This ought to be good.

"I came from a noisy, happy, talkative family," she explained. "We get excited about everything. My husband doesn't get excited about anything. He just works and works—and is dull! I thought I should begin all over again. Here I am, 40 years old, with a new exciting job, and I'm a new Christian—so I need a new husband to go with it all."

I tried hard not to laugh, but I couldn't help but enjoy the entire episode.

"Is your husband a Christian?" I asked.

"Oh, yes, the solid kind."

"Is he a good father?"

"Perfect father."

"Does he love you?"

"He's crazy about me. Gives me flowers and candy. But he is dull!"

"Is he a good provider?"

"Terrific! We have a lovely home !"

I had to say it, "I think you need a new husband!" Harold should have heard that one. "You're right," I continued. "Let him go!"

She clapped her hands, "Oh, I knew you'd see it my way! Everything new!"

"My dear," I repeated, "let him go! I just talked with a dozen gals who'd love a dull husband. Their men chase after butterflies—wine, women and song. How these gals would love a dull man who comes home at 5 P.M., who is a good father and provider. I doubt if they ever saw a box of candy or flowers. These gals would stand in line for a dull guy."

By this time she wasn't too sure where we were going. So I asked, "What kind of childhood did he have?"

"Terrible! Could never please his father."

"Great," I said. "Now he can't please you, even with flowers. What was your family like?"

"Ah, music, laughter, fun, excitement—and noisy." Wistfully she added, "Oh, how I miss that."

"I understand," I told her. "There was nothing dull about my Norwegian family."

We were quiet.

"By the way, did it every occur to you that God put you into his life to give him the joy he never knew?" I asked.

"Oh, no. I never thought of that."

Impulsively, I added, "I just love you! I wish you lived near me so we could have some fun lunches together!"

We quietly prayed that God would speak to her during the next sessions and give her the answers she needed.

"We have to go, but we'll talk later," I promised.

The retreat came to a close and she came to see me. "Margaret, Margaret, I saw it! This guy is terrific! What a man! I've been so blind. I am to give the joy I had in my family to him and our family. Oh, I need this man and he needs me. Guess what? I called him and told him to get ready. Mama mia is coming home! We'll farm out the kids and take off for a fun time."

She chuckled delightedly, "This guy won't know what hit him. Wow! Wait until I tell this dull man how much I love him."

We hugged and laughed together. (The dozen other gals would have to wait!)

"Oh, Mom, I can't believe you!" said Chris.

Our coffee break was over. Chris had errands to run and I had my scraggly garden to clean up. My hands pulled up the dry flower stems that once had filled the garden with bright colors laughing in the sun, and my thoughts flew in a million directions. Old friends of long ago came to mind, once bright and colorful. But when sin walked through the cracks of unthankfulness, bitterness and rebellion followed. Their dried up leaves blow in the winds of winter.

Unthankfulness can open the door to every evil thing. The beginning is subtle, like the children of Israel griping and complaining, and then they turned in rebellion to serve lesser gods and wandered in a dry, barren wilderness. How easy it is for adultery to slip in through the crack of not being thankful for your mate. The eroding sin of covetousness can begin with a crack in the door—not being thankful for the small house, the old car or the used wardrobe.

Mama's message seemed to echo through the years, "Wear your shoes with a thankful heart." Then she would say, "Ja, it iss so simple—it iss yust not always so eassy."

I pulled up the dry, prickly stubble, and raked the garden plot clean. Now Harold could use the tiller to prepare the ground for spring. For a moment I thought of the trees of righteousness God had planted, men and women who stand in the storms of life, planted by the rivers of living water and drinking from the life-giving source of His grace. As they praise Him and thank Him, they are strengthened by His mighty hand, propped up by His mercy.

TO PRAISE AND THANK

Think of a specific reason to praise God today and say it out loud: "I praise God for _____."

OH give thanks to the LORD, for He is good;
    For His lovingkindness is everlasting.
Let the redeemed of the LORD say so
(Psalm 107:1,2a).

---

10 Coconut Pie

"Grammy, I should never have gone to church this morning; in fact, I should have stayed in bed. This is the worst day of my life," said 15-year-old Eric.

"Oh, it can't be that bad," I answered him absent-mindedly. I took the beef roast out of the oven and made the gravy. I called to Shawn, "Come and give these potatoes your mighty arm. Make them nice and fluffy." Adding milk and butter, he beat the potatoes like he played ball.

"Sarah, you may put the ice in the glasses," I continued the countdown to dinner, passing Eric's

problem by. The tables had been set the night before.
"Katie? Where's Katie?"

"I know, I know," she answered, "two salts, two
peppers, two pads of butter, and cream and sugar."

"Now, where is Eric?" I asked. "He can get the
chairs. Dinner will be ready in a minute."

The cars were pulling into the driveway. We'd
be ten in the dining room and six in the breakfast room.

"Do I have to sit with the boys?" Sarah mur-
mured. "My place is always beside Papa."

"I know," I sympathized, "but we have ten
adults, okay? Tell you what, I'll slip your plate by Papa
and we'll squeeze one of us on the corner." Then I
realized there weren't enough chairs. "Eric? Where are
you?" Looking up, I saw his grim expression.

"I told you, Grammy, I never should have gotten
out of bed. It's the worst day of my life." His six-foot
frame showed utter desolation.

Aunt Janice was laughing. "Oh, Eric, nothing can
be that bad." I stirred the gravy; Shawn kept beating;
Chris began to pour lemonade.

"You won't laugh when you hear what happened," continued Eric. "I was sitting in church when I
noticed that my shirt was on backward and that dumb
tag was sticking out in front."

I chuckled! I shouldn't have done that. "It's not
funny, Grammy. Do you realize how humiliating that
is in front of my friends?"

"Oh, I'm sorry, Eric. I know how I felt last Sunday when Katie discovered my shower cap stuck in the
belt of my dress."

"No kidding?"

"Oh, yes. And one time I went to church with one blue shoe and one black."

A new respect showed on Eric's face.

Eric was the picture of despair.
"My favorite pie," he moaned.

"Yeah, but that's not as bad as my day. Anyway, I slipped down in my seat to doodle on the bulletin, anything to keep busy. Then my dumb pencil slipped under a fat lady and when I tried to get it she thought I was fresh. Oh, Grammy, it was awful.

"Then, wouldn't you know it? Communion Sunday, and guess what I did? I spilled the wine and broke the glass.

"I ran out of the church as soon as the benediction was over and ran to the car. I just wanted out! How was I to know that Mama's coconut pie was under the towel? She had put foil around it, then covered it with a towel." He hesitantly added, "I sat on the pie!"

Everything stopped. I stopped stirring the gravy. Shawn stopped beating the potatoes. Chris stopped pouring lemonade. We all yelled at once, "You didn't!"

"Yup, I did!" confessed Eric. "I sat on Mama's fresh coconut pie."

"That was our dessert!"

"Tell me about it!" He was the picture of despair. "My favorite pie," he moaned.

I wrapped my arms around him. He was a V.I.P. to me. Now I understood his sagging spirit, and I wanted to prop him up.

"Don't worry, Eric. You'll forget this in a hundred years from now. That's what my mama told me. Besides, I baked a chocolate cake, just to have as extra."

"Really? Chocolate cake?" he brightened. "That's my next favorite!"

After a good dinner, the worst day in Eric's life came to a close and would ease into the backroads of his mind. The men headed out to sea in the boat. The rest of us took a good Sunday-afternoon nap.

I have an idea Eric's day will be retold to cousins, then grandchildren, down through the years. No one will ever forget the day he sat on the coconut pie!

TO UNDERSTAND

Is there a V.I.P. in your life who needs understanding? What amuses us may be misery to someone else. Sometimes we laugh when we should listen. Sometimes we are tough when we should be tender-hearted.

> Be kind to one another, tender-hearted,
> forgiving each other, just as God in Christ
> also has forgiven you (Ephesians 4:32).

by abandoned joy . . .

---

11 "It's Fun to Be a Child"

During my sister Doris's visit to our beautiful city by the sea, we made a happy decision to take the girls out to lunch. Sarah, then 8, and Kathryn, 6, dressed up, even to lace socks and pocketbooks dangling from their shoulders. This day they were young ladies going out with Grammy and Aunt Doris.

We laughed and talked, enjoying our lunch. For a while Doris and I got involved in adult conversation, but then our attention was drawn to the girls. They looked at each other, giggled, and again became quiet. Without a word their eyes met and they started giggling again. They couldn't stop. We chuckled to ourselves just watching them.

Suddenly Kathryn threw up her hands and with the abandonment of joy exploded, "Oh, it's so fun to be a child!"

Later that night I found myself before a staid, reserved church group. The message I had prepared seemed to lack something and then it came to me: It is pure joy to be a child! I told the story of our lunch giggles and moved into my message with the reminder that *joy is the mark of the child of God.*

Jesus came that our joy might be full, and we are reminded that the joy of the Lord is our strength. How often we confuse happiness with joy. Happiness depends on happenings that are pleasant. For the obedient child of God, there can be joy and peace in the midst of difficult circumstances. Joy is of the spirit.

How the children must have loved Jesus—I can almost hear them laughing and saying, "It's so fun to be a child." He must have laughed with them for He sometimes disregarded the concern of His disciples, and He even encouraged those disciples to become like children.

Older people and children can laugh and giggle together, but we older ones also can let the passing of the years remind us to sometimes become children ourselves again.

We can cut away the sham and pretense, laugh at squirrels scurrying with their nuts, watch noisy bluejays squabble over a crust of bread, cheer the cat who outwitted the dog by climbing a tree, and enjoy the frantic efforts of the frustrated canine hunter. We know that golden autumn leaves aren't for raking alone but also for play. Empty cardboard boxes become mighty fortresses. A magnolia tree becomes a house.

"Grammy, could I have my lunch up here?" asked 4-year-old Kathryn from her "house" in the magnolia tree.

When I was younger I probably would have said, "That's ridiculous!" Now I laugh and say, "Sounds great to me." A tray is hoisted up and the crusts fall to the birds.

> The cotton candy and balloons are part of another day, but we keep cheering. The game of life goes on.

"Maybe I could take my nap up here?" she asks next.

"I'm afraid you'll fall out, but we'll have a party later," I decide.

"I hate naps! Only Grammy likes naps." How true that one is!

So when life becomes competitive, the market place seems like a jungle, and I need a little proppin' up, I'll try to stop long enough to hear two joyful little girls giggling, "It's so fun to be a child!" I may even take one of them someplace.

Another day brought another moment to savor.

"Papa, you promised to take us to the County Fair," reminded Kathryn. She never forgets a promise.

So it came to pass that poor old Grammy and Papa walked endless miles to see blue ribbon winners, stomp through tons of sawdust, listen to shrieking vendors, and stand spellbound while Eric and Kathryn were whirled around and around up in the middle of the wild blue yonder. Cotton candy, hot dogs and cokes filled up the empty places.

Harold and I found a sitting place and watched the crowd forget their cares and become children again, just for a day. Tomorrow with its toil would come soon enough, but today all were children with balloons and stuffed animals, apple taffy and popcorn.

I read someplace where a child begged his mother for a balloon.

"You don't need a balloon," she answered.

An old man sitting on a park bench bought a balloon and gave it to the child, saying, "Lady, the day of balloons passes too quickly."

So it is with fairs, ball games and cheerleaders. Today is their day. Too soon it passes.

Heather, a student at Brown University, isn't interested in balloons anymore. She's now making life-changing choices. But the memories of balloons and ferris wheels and cotton candy won't go away.

Chad, a freshman at Gordon College yells with pleasure, "Got a B, Grammy." The competition continues. "Got a part in the school play. And I'm on the soccer team."

The cotton candy and the balloons are part of another day, but we keep cheering as the game of life goes on.

Well, if Kathryn wants to go to the fair next year, I'm sure we'll go. You are a V.I.P. in our lives, Kathryn. We'll go for one more ride into the blue, one more hot dog, cotton candy or balloon. Too soon, this moment will be gone and the youngest will take her place in the game of life.

Isn't it strange that Jesus should tell us to become like children to enter the Kingdom of Heaven? I wonder if God doesn't sometimes long to hear His children say, "Oh, Father, it's so fun to be Your child!"

TO BE JOYFUL

It is amazing how joy can be contagious. And how it props up the leanin' side! So let's be joyful! Wait! Joy cannot be demanded or determined by our desire to be joyful. Joy is the result of a continuous commitment to our relationship with Christ.

> Walk by the Spirit, and you will not carry
> out the desire of the flesh . . . the fruit of
> the Spirit is love, joy, peace, patience, kind-
> ness, goodness, faithfulness, gentleness,
> self-control (Galatians 5:16-23).

12 Going
Home

From the window of the plane, the city of Toronto looked like a Christmas wonder. The streets appeared to be lined with trees filled with Christmas lights. The snow fell gently at first, then it turned into a spectacular windy blizzard with the reflected lights dancing in the snow.

The Holiday Inn never looked so good to me. I unpacked my suitcases, pressed my clothes, and decided to take the elevator to the Chestnut Tree restaurant. There the hostess seated me by the window. What fun it was to observe travelers enveloped in fur hats, coats and boots as they braced against the wind. It was the end of the day and their steps were turned toward home.

The next morning Ralph Bradley, chaplain of "100 Huntley Street," met me for breakfast. Then we headed through the snow and ice toward the television studio and old friends. I had been to Toronto several times.

As soon as we arrived the preparations began for the countdown to a live show. With Rod directing, cameras moved about like robots. Johanna seemed to be everywhere at once, and lovely Myra made her guests at ease as she interviewed people from every walk of life. Cal was set for his theological commentary and I was seated beside David, the president and host of the show. He is bigger than life with a heart that embraces the globe. Hand in hand, he and his lovely wife Norma Jean enfold the world around them.

Countdown! The camera was on and David introduced me with the theme for the week: "First We Have Coffee." I began to share the story of my book which had that same title. It originated with my Norwegian mama who prefaced dealing with every crisis in life by saying just that: "First we have coffee."

When a lonely immigrant with fears and tears would come to our house in Canada, Mama would say, "Come, sit down, sit down. First we have coffee, then we talk." While she prepared the coffee she would think about what might be the problem and spin a story that would give a solution.

After coffee she would ask, "Now, what was it?"

"Oh, it was nothing," the satisfied guest would answer.

"But, Mama, why didn't you let her tell you her problem?" we would ask.

"Oh, ja, sometimes it is good to tell; sometimes it is good to wait. Could be tomorrow she has the answer. It is better to tell it to Jesus. He is the only one who can help."

Our gracious hostess tucked me in
on the sofa beside an open fire.
No tractor ride for me.

I returned to the studio the next day accompanied by my son Ralph, who would also be a guest. He would be sharing his story of spiritual struggle and of how God turned his steps toward home. In *Lena* I had written about his journey and about how my dear friend Lena would prop up my leanin' side when my heart was aching.

With quiet gentleness Ralph told of the seeds of rebellion that had been planted in his young heart when he saw the injustice and hypocrisy of "so-called Christians."

"I believed a lie," he said. "I judged the church by a few. When I met Jesus and yielded my life to Him, all the hurt, bitterness, hatred and rebellion left. I was freed by God's power. All those years I could have had this peace, love and forgiveness. But I believed a lie.

"Don't let Satan cheat you," he urged the audience. "Turn your life over to God's redeeming love."

It was a moving moment and we all felt the presence of God. I realized in a new way how carefully we must walk before our children, to take the time to listen to their hurts and fears, to be a leaning post, not a stumbling block.

While we were guests of "100 Huntley Street," Ralph and I had the pleasure of visiting a 350-acre farm with a beautifully restored home that had been built in the 1800s. Bruce Stam took Ralph with him on an old tractor and they rode all over the snow-clad hills and valleys. Twenty-three horses were out to pasture, then led into the barn for the night and cared for by the Stams' young daughter.

Valerie Stam, our gracious hostess, tucked me in on the sofa beside an open fire. No tractor ride for me.

Ralph is an avid sportsman, and he spotted seven deer and a bobcat in the valley. I was happy to be by the fire.

When we gathered around Valerie's beautiful table that evening, I couldn't help but marvel at the grace of God. One moment we were strangers, the next a family—a part of God's wonderful family, one in Christ. Three beautiful daughters laughed and joked with Ralph—which wasn't surprising; after all, he has four children of his own. And we all enjoyed the pumpkin soup, roast chicken, homemade bread and apple pie.

After a week in Toronto, I was on my way home. My heart was full. I had watched humble, dedicated people living simple lifestyles, pouring out the compassion of Christ to a needy world.

I thought particularly of Diane, my dynamic friend and a special guest on the program. She described the challenge they had accepted which resulted in some 25,000 toys being sent to Uganda, with "Jesus Loves You." The leader of that country had thanked God that after twenty years Christmas came to Uganda.

I recalled that Isaiah 58 had stirred a response in David, the president of the show. He was challenged to feed the hungry and take back the streets for God. We heard of one man who brought soup and sandwiches to the street people.

The program sponsors summer camps for children from every ethnic group. Their next challenge is to reach out to the Russian children who have to be kept indoors because of the contaminated earth from the Chernobyl disaster.

I also warmly remembered God's unfailing grace in the life of my son Ralph. It had a powerful effect, really proppin' up my leanin' side.

TO REMEMBER

Remembering God's faithfulness in past situations is a wonderful proppin' up exercise.

> Remember the former days, when after being enlightened, you endured a great conflict of sufferings (Hebrews 10:32).

Remember how He pulled you through, how He propped you up, empowered you to go on "joyfully"?

> Therefore, do not throw away your confidence, which has great reward. For you have need of endurance, so that when you have done the will of God, you may receive what was promised (Hebrews 10:32,35,36).

13 Sunday Dinners

I don't know how it happens. Every Sunday I say, "I have to leave right after church to get the dinner on the table," so how is it that I am always one of the last to leave?

Maybe Harold has the answer: "Do you have to talk to everyone in church?"

As soon as I get home, I change into a comfortable dress with short sleeves. I can't work with long sleeves. Then I tie on a big apron and pull the roast out of the oven to make gravy.

Mama used to say, "The only reason for Saturday is to get ready for Sunday." With Saturday-night baths taken, shoes polished and in a row, Sunday school lessons done and a penny tied in the corner of a handkerchief, we were ready for Sunday on Saturday night. Then Mama went into action. The Sunday dinner was the highlight meal of the week—also, we never knew how many people Papa would bring home. God and Mama stayed prepared. Mama did her part and God did the stretching. There was always enough.

My Norwegian mama set the table Saturday night and made all the Sunday preparations, putting everything in order before she took her Saturday-night bath. Then she put on the coffeepot. Dressed in her long flannel nightgown and robe, she called Papa from his study and they had a quiet cup of coffee with rye bread and cheese before going to bed. Together they would ask God's blessing on the Lord's day. No wonder Sunday was special!

Now it was me taking the roast out of the oven. Often, when I have both hands full, Ralph sneaks up behind me and unties my apron, a trick he began when he was about 4 years old. Just try cooking with apron strings flopping around. As soon as I get the apron tied, another "young-un" slips around to do his trick.

Then we go into high gear! Everyone has something to do. The table, set the night before, has to have finishing touches—ice, butter, etc.

One particular Sunday, Uncle Jack's car as usual pulled up into the driveway. Still erect and handsome at 83, Harold's brother moved slowly to the front door.

There is something special about faithful people. Uncle Jack won't make the morning headlines, but when he faithfully intercedes each day for all his relatives, he gets the attention of the Throne Room of God. With no immediate family of his own, he remembers all the birthdays in the family, and when the church doors open, he is there. Pastors and people come and go, but Uncle Jack comes to church to worship God—he is not moved by temporary circumstances.

Another car pulled up this particular Sunday and Ralph's cousin Steve and his family piled out. Young Benjamin and Paul usually collaborate with Kathryn in their version of "Mission Impossible," and Beverly, Steve's wife, usually has something cooked up with Chris.

> "There was this neat island
> and we decided to go out to it.
> Before we realized it the tide was out
> and we were stuck."

Around the bend came Peter Stam in his red T-Bird, followed by Shawn and Eric in a red jeep. Katie had decided to ride with "Uncle Pete" in his new car. Sarah came with "Aunt Mary" and the boys gave a whoop when they saw their favorite rolls. One Sunday one young-un' got left in the parking lot. We forgot to count.

"Put four more places someplace," I called out. "Shawn has a new family from church coming."

The family arrived.

"Two pots of coffee, Harold, no decaf. We need all the help we can get. Uncle Pete, how about a mighty right to these potatoes? It's a good way to get rid of life's frustrations—beating the potatoes!"

Shawn introduced the new family, a friend and classmate Terry, then Brandy, a college junior, and the parents Jeff and Joan. Within moments they blended into the family with bonds of love, and somehow I couldn't imagine life without them.

Everyone gathered for the blessing and each found his or her place. Sure enough, the mashed potatoes stretched, the gravy seemed unending, and the serving dishes went round and round. Katie managed to slip into the dining room to be sure her table hadn't missed anything. Steve and Ralph, more like brothers than double first cousins (one of Harold's brothers had married one of my sisters), kept everyone in stitches with wild fishing and hunting stories.

Back and forth the stories rolled.

"Remember the barbecue cookout?" Steve was in rare form. "We decided to go fishing and promised the girls we'd be home for the barbecue. There was this neat island and we decided to go out to it. Before we realized it the tide was out and we were stuck. At least Shawn had sense enough to bring a frying pan and some butter and crackers, so we built a fire, and fried fish, but it kept getting later and later."

"We were ready to call the Coast Guard." Chris and Beverly had their own version. "We knew you were in trouble, and the cookout was ruined!"

"We had to wait for the tide so we could get the boat off the island," Steve continued. "We got home about midnight. No barbecue!"

"I guess we'll never live that one down," Ralph added, shaking his head.

While the stories continued, the girls helped to clean the table. We were ready for two pots of coffee and Chris's famous pies: pecan and coconut. Eric didn't go near those pies.

Harold told the new friends about the time Kathryn and Sarah invited another new family, from New Jersey, visiting our church for the first time. "Everyone comes home to Grammy's house on Sunday," she urged. And Harold reminded us, they came too.

When I am traveling, Chris has Sunday dinner at her house, and when Sarah and Kathryn grow up, Papa and Grammy will come to them for Sunday dinner. It's a promise!

In New England, Jan and Jud open their home to students, faculty, staff, and endless friends and strangers. All around the world God's family is made one in His love.

One Sunday, just as we were seating eighteen people, the phone rang.

"Are you busy?"

"Not really. We were just seating our family for Sunday dinner," I said.

Silence.

And then a wistful voice on the other end said, "Oh, I didn't know anyone had Sunday dinner any more. We used to, but it was so long ago."

Sunday dinner is a time when the cares of the week are left behind, when wounded spirits are refreshed with laughter, and when children and adults are together. It is a time when love is stretched, joy is multiplied, and sorrows are lessened. In our day the famine is not so much for food, but it is the famine of the spirit of fellowship. We need to prop each other up!

The Sunday dinner was over, the dishes done, the kitchen clean. I grabbed Eric to take out the garbage. (Mama's rules don't change.) The men discussed plans to go out in the boat. Mary fed her dog. Uncle Jack was happy to go home to peace and quiet, and Harold headed for his leather chair.

Ah, Chris and I put our feet up and read the paper, then took a Sunday nap.

Sarah says, "I just love Sunday."

And I answer, "So do I, Sarah. So do I."

TO CREATE FELLOWSHIP

Take the time to prepare and share a meal with family and friends. It will make them feel like V.I.P.s, even if your house is "not ready," and you don't feel like you have much to offer. It is the familiar fellowship that one feels with the breaking of bread that props up the leanin' side!

And breaking bread from house to house, they were taking their meals together with gladness and sincerity of heart, praising God, and having favor with all the people (Acts 2:46,47).

14 No Place to Go

"Guess what? We had a substitute teacher for our English class today and she taught us how to meditate," Shawn told his mother.

"She did what? Since when does meditation have anything to do with English?"

"I don't know, Mom, but when someone talks about spirit guides and some of those other weird things, I get very uneasy."

"What did you do?"

"I just quietly thought about some of the Scripture verses I knew, and I prayed for my friends. I was

95

worried about them because I know that we become what we think."

"Well, Shawn, I'm glad you told me, and I'll try to use wisdom when I approach the principal. After all, I'm an English teacher, and I'll just ask what meditation, spirit guides and the occult have to do with English."

As Harold and I heard about the experiences of our grandchildren, we were increasingly concerned for parents and for their need for godly wisdom in dealing with the subtle introduction of ideas that would lead our children away from the one true God.

One night as I was coming out of a steakhouse where I had spoken to some Christian educators, I noticed a young man whom I recognized as a waiter. He was sitting in a corner.

Another employee asked, "Aren't you through yet?"

He replied, "Oh, yes, but I have no place to go."

I was reminded of a teacher I knew who had visited one of her honor-roll students and seen his tragic home situation. With dirty dishes, clothing, broken bottles and trash strewn everywhere, there was not one clear spot for the student to study. She marveled that the boy even got to school!

The young waiter's "no place to go" haunted me, and I wondered if perhaps his home was filled with broken bottles—and broken people.

In my school days, a student from a broken home would have had a chance to hear at school the story of Joseph in prison and how he became the prime minister, or of David, a shepherd boy who became a king. The student would have heard of the prophet Daniel's trust in God when Daniel was thrown into the lion's den. There also would have been a good chance that a teacher would tell the Christmas story, and the Easter story. A child would have discovered a place to come home to—the very heart of God. Just one small candle in a classroom might have been enough for a broken life to have someplace to go. The courts blew out the candle.

> "Oh, Grammy," Eric objected,
> "let Sarah do it."
> *"Let Sarah do it"?* I thought.
> *Well, I'll give him a piece of my mind later.*
> *I'll fix him.*

Every heart yearns for some place to go. In the desperate times that come to us all we have just such a place—the heart of God. We can find it in the Word of God. The psalmist cries out, "Thy Word have I hid in my heart." He is asking God to "prop me up according to Thy Word."

I was reminded again of the lonely waiter when one day I asked 15-year-old Eric how he managed at school. "Do you know kids who use drugs?"

"Sure," he answered, "but I just stick with my basketball team and a few friends. Believe me, I don't think it's cool to use drugs or liquor. Most of the time I stick with Dad and Shawn. We have more fun than anyone, just going to games, fishing, boating or hunting. Now that's cool!"

He had a place to go.

I was reminded of how important that time with his Dad was to him one Sunday following church. I asked Eric to go with some new visitors who were coming home for dinner and didn't know the way to our house.

"Oh, Grammy," he objected, "let Sarah do it."

"Let Sarah do it"? I thought. *Well, I'll give Eric a piece of my mind later. I'll fix him.*

By the time I got around to "fixing" Eric, though, I was calmer, cooler and more collected. "Eric, I'm curious. Why did you want Sarah to go with the visitors?"

"It's this way, Grammy. I always ride with Dad after church. Mom takes the van and Dad and I ride in the jeep. He always has something to say, and I don't want to miss it! Besides, he's fun to be with!"

For a moment I was quiet and wondered how many times my heavenly Father had something to say and I missed it. Besides that, He is great to be with, for "in His presence is fullness of joy" (Psalm 16:11).

I just hugged Eric a little harder and realized again how proppin' up the leanin' side comes in many ways. Relationships need constant proppin' in order to grow strong. Eric found a place of strength with his Dad. (I never did get around to "fixing" him—in fact, he "fixed" me.)

We need to know who (and what) is proppin' up our children—from whom (and what) they are learning.

This is the hour for us to prop up the leanin' sides of school, church and government leaders who stand tall in the war of values. If the enemy wins the battle for our children, we will live as slaves to a godless society where there is no final authority except tyranny.

Proper proppin' begins in our families, with each member living out their values, loving each other unconditionally and lighting a candle to spark the faith given to everyone.

TO LEARN

Share this prayer with someone important in your life today:

Make me know Thy ways, O LORD;
Teach me Thy paths.
Lead me in Thy Truth and teach me,
For Thou art the God of my salvation;
For Thee I wait all the day (Psalm 25:4,5).

---

15 The Cinnamon Rolls

It was one of those grey, rainy, dreary days that needed a little proppin' up. The leanin' sides seemed weighted down with a cloud of doom.

"I'll bake bread and cinnamon rolls," I thought. Kneading the dough with a fury, I could at least do something, even if I couldn't change the weather. While the dough was rising, I decided to check my office and tackle a pile of mail in need of attention. I couldn't change the outside, but I could clear my desk. So I busied myself sorting papers, mail, and my writing on yellow pads.

Oh, the bread! I almost forgot. I had left the dough in a large bowl sitting on a chair that I'd placed over the warmth of the floor heat register. On cold, rainy days dough needs some help.

I caught it in time and it was perfect. So I formed three loaves and rolled the rest out for cinnamon rolls. Covering the dough with melted butter, brown sugar, nuts, raisins and cinnamon, I rolled it like a jelly roll and started slicing. There they were. The three rolls of bread and three pans of cinnamon rolls were covered to rise again.

I had time to run out to my office in back of the garage and write for an hour; then I would put the rolls in to bake. Harold would be ready for a cup of coffee after all his errands in the cold rain.

In what seemed a very short time, I heard the car pull into the driveway so I ran to the kitchen. The rolls were ready and I put them into the oven.

"What a day!" Harold shook his raincoat and hung it up to dry. "It's so cold—almost feels like snow." I put the coffeepot on.

"What do I smell? Wow! Cinnamon rolls!"

The cold, rainy day didn't seem so gloomy.

Thirty minutes later we settled down to have coffee and rolls when suddenly we heard a door open and, "Hey, Grammy! What do I smell? Way to go!"

Sarah poured milk—and Ralph yelled, "Who stole the middle roll?" We all started to laugh. Of course, no one but Eric!

"So, what's so big about the middle roll?" Eric asked as he poured another glass of milk.

Ralph chuckled. "When I was just a little kid, the standing rule was that no one, but no one, got the middle roll except Daddy One day, Janice asked, 'How old do you have to be to get the middle roll?' and Grammy said, 'As long as Daddy is on this earth he gets the middle roll.'" Harold just smirked—and nodded.

"When we asked why," Ralph continued, "Grammy said, 'Because he is number one in this family, and Daddy believes that the raisins and nuts run a race to the middle, and he likes raisins and nuts.' "

"Don't let Eric get those rolls!" I called. Eric just grinned with a bewitching, "I love you, Grammy."

All through the years the middle roll remained a family joke. Now Eric broke the rule, and at least three more rolls were missing.

The bread was ready to eat by this time. Sarah could have her favorite—homemade bread. I reminded her how I liked the end slices, and told her about the day I came home from school and sliced six ends. Mama knew I did it, and it was our joke.

The coffee was hot, real butter melted fast on those hot rolls, and the milk jug was getting low. We were all feeling better. Silly stories from the past were told and retold, like the time Eric ate a jar of dill pickles, the time Katie hid a box of chocolates under the bed, and now the middle cinnamon roll. The day remained grey and cold outside, but the warm kitchen with the fragrance of bread propped up our leanin' sides.

It's the little things that linger on the backroads of our memory. We brace ourselves to face the crises of life, but somehow we remember the grey days of wounded spirits that got a little proppin' up from a small gesture of love.

Then it was time for Ralph, Eric and Sarah to leave, and they braced themselves to run to the car, carrying warm bread and cinnamon rolls home to Chris.

"Don't let Eric get those rolls!" I called.

Eric just grinned with a bewitching, "I love you, Grammy," and I didn't care how many rolls he ate.

Someday, when the grey, cold, stormy days come stealing into their lives creating gloom and doubt, perhaps someone will remember the middle cinnamon roll, and remember how the raisins and nuts race for the center. Through the corridors of memory they'll hear Harold say, "Who got the middle roll?"

TO CHOOSE CHEER

How much do we do for our V.I.P.'s out of a sense of duty? Determine to be a cheerful giver today.

> Let each one do as he has purposed in
> his heart; not grudgingly or under com-
> pulsion; for God loves a cheerful giver
> (2 Corinthians 9:7).

by gentle love . . .

---

16 Jimmy's Song

While some people race over the highways of life in the challenging pursuit of power or pleasure, others take a country lane and walk a little slower. I have noticed that often, when the end of the road is reached, the ones who move in the slow lane win the race of life.

My friend, Jimmy, walked soft-like through life. When overcome with grief over the loss of his father, he retreated into a lonely world of doubt and unbelief. How could a good God take his best friend?

Music was Jimmy's great love and his understanding family provided a soundproof room where he played recordings of the great artists. Jimmy's beautiful tenor voice blended in unison with the performers until it was difficult to tell the difference. Since an audience intimidated him, he sang alone for hours.

One day a soft-spoken, gentle girl named Margaret heard him singing and she became his audience. During the days of music a friendship formed; then he sang the love songs, from his heart right into her heart. "Be my love," he sang, and she became his sweetheart wife. Through her gentle ways she shared her unshakable faith in God, and took him by the heart to lead him back to the faith of his childhood, to the reality of God's love for him.

"I'll never be lonely again. God loves me, and my beautiful angel loves me," Jimmy said.

Harold and I visited Margaret and Jimmy in their cozy home, and we drank tea together. Then Jimmy gave us a concert. He blended his voice with a recording of Ed Lyman singing the songs of faith, and the two voices sounded as one. It was one of those wondrous moments that come, never to return again.

Through the years our paths separated and we didn't hear Jimmy sing again, although news came across the miles of how he worked faithfully every day.

"I have to take care of my angel," he said.

He not only had the practical qualities of faithfulness and dependability, but he also moved through life with the courtesy of a Southern gentleman.

Hand in hand, Margaret and Jimmy served God and people faithfully. The living Christ who enables us to do the impossible gave Jimmy a new boldness and love for his Saviour. He shared his gift with the lonely people in nearby nursing homes, singing of his faith in a loving God, and he shared the story of God's great salvation. From his heart of love, he reached out to lonely prisoners behind bars, singing and preaching about God's freedom through Christ. He was a frequent soloist at his home church, and at office Christmas parties he was the special feature, singing and leading the singing.

His wife wrote us about his heart for evangelism, his longing to share the love of God in music and words. He continued to reach into the lonely places singing the songs of faith and hope, bringing God's amazing grace that went beyond wheelchairs and prison bars.

> Because of her faith,
> Jimmy's faith had acquired
> a new boldness to share God's love
> in words and music.

Then one day God took Jimmy Home. The music was stilled and the world became a lonelier place without him. "My sweetheart has gone Home. How I miss him!" wrote Margaret.

I reminded her of how God had used her to put the song of salvation into his heart. She was there to prop up his leanin' side. Because of her faith, Jimmy's faith had acquired a new boldness to share God's love in words and music. Because of Jimmy's music, some who were lonely now have hope, some who were prisoners now have a new freedom, some who were discouraged now have new faith—and by faith the song goes on.

He was there to prop up their leanin' sides!

Perhaps God needed an extra tenor in the heavenly choir and sent an angel to bring him Home. If we walk a little slower, a little more soft-like, it may be that we will hear Jimmy's song: "Amazing grace, how sweet the sound . . . "

TO LOVE

Take a second look at someone you consider an "independent" or possibly a "loner." Perhaps that person's world is lonely, filled with unbelief and fear. You can prop him or her up with a little gentle love.

> Love is patient, love is kind . . . is not
> provoked, does not take into account
> a wrong suffered, does not rejoice in
> unrighteousness, but rejoices with the
> truth; bears all things, believes all things,
> hopes all things, endures all things
> (1 Corinthians 13:4-8).

17 Desert Storm, 1991

"Papa, Papa, did you hear the news? War has begun!"

These were the children who knew nothing of war. We did! With heavy hearts, we watched the news and came to the final realization: Diplomacy had failed. Yes, the war had begun in spite of all the diplomatic overtures during the last months, and we had to face the reality.

As Katie brought up the subject, my eyes met Harold's. This was serious. We knew it was best to talk about it openly. We knew that would help to prop up the children's leanin' sides—and ours!

"Will you go to war, Papa?"

"No, Katie, I'm too old."

"How old are you?"

"Seventy-eight."

"Wow! That is old!"

Katie was content. Her world was safe. She picked up her doll and began to play. She knew that "Swenson lunches" with Papa were still intact.

It was Shawn who continued to talk.

"I've been reading a lot about the Middle East, and it is unreal what happened to Kuwait, a small defenseless country that Saddam plundered and raped. If he got away with that, then he'd head for Saudi Arabia." Then sounding like a preacher he concluded, "But the final objective is Israel."

"Is this the beginning of Armageddon, Papa?" Eric was very serious.

"I don't think so," Harold replied carefully, "but it is certainly leading up to the final war according to Bible prophecy."

He continued to explain that most students of prophecy seemed to think this would be a short war, and then after Saddam's defeat there would be a temporary peace in the volatile Middle East. He thought the final war would come later. That would be Armageddon.

"I heard we are fighting for oil," our usually bubbly Sarah joined earnestly.

Her comment began a discussion of Israel and how it became a homeland for the Jews in 1948. For two thousand years they had been scattered among the nations, yet they retained their identity. Harold explained that ever since the return of the Jews to their homeland, the prophetic clock has been ticking toward the final hour, the coming of the Messiah.

All eyes were fastened on him as he continued to answer the urgent questions. He talked of the Jews coming to a wasteland and making the desert bloom like a rose, and he spoke of how Russian Jews are streaming into Israel.

> "Papa, is this the end of the world?
> I want to get married and have
> children before the end of the world."
> Katie has a way of coming
> right to her point.

It was one of those times when Sunday dinner-table conversation flowed freely back and forth. I was reminded of how I used to listen to missionaries and theologians around our kitchen table in the second-floor flat in Chicago.

I was supposed to be asleep, but I would listen.

Late into the night the discussions on doctrine and prophecy continued.

"According to the Bible, God will bring the Jews to Palestine and they will have a homeland."

"How can that be? After so many years, what could ever happen that could bring the Jews back to Palestine?"

"Ja, that is a mystery. I wonder if we will see that in our lifetimes?"

I heard the pages of the Bibles rustle, and Mama's guests reading from the prophets of old, Daniel, Ezekiel and Isaiah, then reading from the New Testament, to the last book, the Revelation. Then I would hear Mama say it was time for coffee. The Bibles were put aside and I would fall asleep wondering if Jesus would come in the night.

"Grammy," Shawn was speaking to me and I was brought back to reality. "Grammy, I'm 18—and I could go to war." There was gravity in his voice and we all began to feel great emotion.

"I'm glad I'm only 15." Eric was grim. "But I'd hate it if Shawn and Chad had to go to war."

"Papa, is this the end of the world? I want to get married and have children before the end of the world. I know Jesus is coming but I want to get married first." Katie, 9 years old, has a way of coming right to her point.

Our Sunday dinner conversation was longer than usual that day, but it was a proppin'-up time, a time to remind us all that we belong to God and no matter what happens, though there be wars and rumors of wars, earthquakes, and disasters in strange places, we belong to God.

Eric gathered up his size 13 basketball shoes, slipped his jacket over his shoulders, and reached his long arms to give a hug. I felt a lump in my heart. He was so young and so vulnerable, but I remembered, not helpless. God is a very present help in time of trouble.

I turned to the girls, my beautiful girls. "We have to figure out some special day to go out to lunch and the mall," I told them. A quick hug and they were headed for the car.

Ralph lingered a moment. "Here I am expanding my business—and this world is so crazy and uncertain! One thing I know is that every move I've ever made has been a step of faith. We can't operate on fear. It must be on faith in God."

Harold hugged him hard and long, this special son, and reminded him that Jesus never fails. We all stand together on the promises of God and His never-failing love. It was a special moment of proppin' up the leanin' sides.

We closed the door for the night.

TO TALK

As we speak "the truth in love, we . . . grow up in all aspects" in Christ (Ephesians 4:15). Encourage the V.I.P.s in your life today by allowing them to talk and by trusting them with the truth—in love.

by significant gathering . . .

18 The Call

"My gourmet Saturday-night-special soup is so scrumptious you won't believe it," I told Chris over the phone. "Why don't you and Ralph come over? I followed the recipe exactly—well, almost exactly."

Chris laughed on the other end of the line and said, "I'll believe that when I see it—you following a recipe! What is it?"

"Cream of broccoli soup," I began enthusiastically, "only I added extra carrots and less broccoli. With a half pound of cheese it ought to be good. Besides, I baked bread today, and cinnamon rolls for our Sunday breakfast."

So the plans were made. Then a short time later they were abruptly changed—again by phone.

"Have you heard? Tom got the call! We're meeting at Frank's home to give Tom and Beth our support."

"Of course, we'll be there," I said.

The phones rang across town: "Tom got the call. Be at Frank's house!"

It was decided that Ralph and Chris would come by for my gourmet soup first. At least for Chris and me it was super-scrumptious. As for Harold and Ralph, a meal isn't a meal without mashed potatoes and meat balls. The bread and cinnamon rolls made up for "just soup."

Our main concern and topic of conversation was Tom's call. Tom, a trained Marine helicopter pilot was a missionary candidate for the Moody Aviation Missions. Within a few months he would be entering the final stages of preparation. Then he got the call to report for duty in the Persian Gulf. At first he and Beth were overcome with despair. He didn't want to leave Beth and their young child alone.

The cars began to come. They filled Frank's driveway and lined the street as the friends gathered. Punch, popcorn, cakes and plates of cookies appeared out of nowhere.

Young couples and single young people came looking vulnerable; elders and leaders came looking concerned. Harold and I were the only "old folks." Few had passed this way before.

"Don't tell me not to cry," Tom's voice broke. "Don't tell me not to grieve. Don't tell me not to be afraid. I am afraid. Believe me, I don't feel like a mighty warrior, dressed for battle.

"These past few years I have concentrated on being a loving husband, and I just can't adjust emotionally from changing diapers to flying killer missions. My mind and emotions, my entire being, is in turmoil.

"I was well trained. I know my job and I have many men under me and I am confident of my ability. It's just that all my thinking has been on life-saving flying missions.

"I'm not afraid to die; but I am afraid to leave Beth and Caleb. How will they manage?"

He stood a little taller
and the fear was slinking away
into the shadows.
Faith was winning.

We watched the faces of the young people around us, some of whom had survived Vietnam. No one dared to venture any pat answers. There were none. The young men, usually full of jokes, or bent on arguing the virtues of their favorite team, or adding a few inches to the big fish that got away, were suddenly silent.

Then slowly came the words of support to prop up the leanin' sides.

"Hey, Tom, count on me to look after Beth. If anything needs fixing, I'll do it. Keep my number handy."

"We'll try to find someone to stay with Beth and help with Caleb."

"Hey, Beth, if you have car trouble, you know my number."

We listened quietly. Across the room the words came. "Don't be afraid, Tom and Beth. I am with you and I will give you strength and help and hold you up in your time of need."

Something special seemed to be happening. Praise to God for His past blessings was renewing faith for today. We were reminded of how God took care of baby Caleb when he fell out of a second story window. Protective bushes had broken the fall. Praises to God began to flow, and the promises of God came with assurance.

I looked at Tom, God's V.I.P., a chosen vessel who had just had a change of orders. He stood a little taller, and the fear was slinking away into the shadows. Faith was winning.

My thoughts were moving in many directions, but my heart was fixed on thanks to God for the friends who had gathered around Tom and Beth that Saturday night. We watched the dreaded foe—fear, the darkness of doubt, discouragement and defeat—slip around to the back roads when prayer and praise put the enemy to flight.

Before the night came to a close, we joined hands and hearts to sing, "Bind us together with cords of love that cannot be broken."

Looking around the crowded room, Tom said, "I can't believe you would all come out like this. You'll never know what you have done for us."

Then it was time to go. Cars pulled out of the driveway and away from the curbs, headed for home.

The next day was Sunday. During the morning service, Tom, commanding and handsome in his officer's uniform, and Beth were called up to the front to kneel at the altar—their commissioning to the mission field, the Persian Gulf.

The days and weeks flew by, but to Beth it seemed like an eternity of waiting.

"Has he gone yet?"

"I don't know. He's training in some desert—supposed to go next week.

Next week came. "No, there's been a delay for some reason."

The friends rallied and Beth was not alone.

Then one day Tom came home. "The mission I was to go on was canceled. We're not going to Desert Storm."

Then the war was over!

"Well, what about your job?"

"I don't know, but I'm trusting the Lord to supply our need."

He did!

Tom was given a better job, and now his young family is serving the Lord, knowing that the same God who cared for them in the past will continue to provide guidance for the future.

The war is over, but the conflict continues. Nations rise and fall, but God remains unchanged. His Word is settled for the child of God who is in His care.

God's people respond by proppin' up the leanin' sides, gathering around with both faith and works. They go together.

Trust and obey;
There is no other way . . .

EPILOGUE

Thumbing through the *Decision* magazine of February 1991, I happened to see an article by the late Alan Redpath, "Living in the Light of His Return." He said:

The hope of Jesus' coming again was the inspiration of the early church. It motivated them as they went out to witness. Today we need a revival of that hope in our hearts.

Living in the "Light of His Return"—in the light of eternity—a Christian has no room for slackness in service.

I was reminded of Miss Sophia, a Norwegian immigrant in Papa's church. She was wrinkled and stooped with the years of hard living, yet the glory of the Lord shone in her eyes.

All week she toiled as a maid in other people's homes, but on Sunday she stood tall as a child of the King.

119

In the 1930s, Papa's evening service abounded with the joy of music—the string band, the choir, duets and quartets. Music was the language of the soul.

Papa had a habit of asking if anyone had a favorite chorus or hymn. We all knew what Miss Sophia would request. Every Sunday night she asked for "Glad Day! Glad Day!"

> Jesus may come today—Glad day! Glad day!
> And I would see my Friend;
> Dangers and troubles would end
> If Jesus should come today.
> Glad day! Glad day!

We didn't have to look it up—everyone knew Miss Sophia's song. Monday, she would be scrubbing floors, but the song in her heart remained "Glad day! Jesus may come today."

I was a teenager, but I sensed a desire to live as if Jesus would come that day, so I would request, "Living for Jesus, a life that is true."

The '30s passed. Jesus didn't come. Miss Sophia went Home to be with the Lord. The church sang, "Glad day! Jesus may come today." He had come for Miss Sophia.

Now, we who were then young have grown old, but every so often I still sing, "Glad Day! Jesus may come today!"

Living in the light of His return is motivation for holy living, and it creates in us a burning desire to share God's love with others.

I want to keep living for Jesus, a life that is true.

Don't you?

Enjoy More of Margaret Jensen's Delightful Bestsellers!

Quantity		Total
———	**FIRST WE HAVE COFFEE** – Poignant, humorous stories about growing up in an immigrant Norwegian Baptist pastor's home, where Mama's words, "First we have coffee," served as a prelude to all her problem-solving. ISBN 0-89840-050-3/$7.99	$ ——
———	**PAPA'S PLACE** – True stories about life lived at Papa's Place, showing how even a difficult father can be understood and accepted. ISBN 0-89840-175-5/$7.99	$ ——
———	**A NAIL IN A SURE PLACE: Holding On When You Want to Let Go** – Unforgettable characters from Margaret's childhood and adolescence who inspired her with their endurance, godliness and unsung commitment to others by allowing God to use them as a "nail in a sure place." ISBN 0-89840-250-6/$7.99	$ ——

Your Christian bookseller should have these products in stock. Please check with him before using this "Shop by Mail" Form.

Send completed order form to: **HERE'S LIFE PUBLISHERS, INC.**
P. O. Box 1576
San Bernardino, CA 92402-1576

Name _____

Address _____

State _____ Zip _____

❑ Payment enclosed
   (check or money order only)

❑ Visa   ❑ Mastercard

#_____

Expiration Date _____

Signature _____

**For faster service,
call toll free:
1-800-950-4457**

ORDER TOTAL	$ ——
SHIPPING and HANDLING ($1.50 for one item, $0.50 for each additional. Do not exceed $4.00.)	$ ——
APPLICABLE SALES TAX (CA 6.75%)	$ ——
TOTAL DUE	$ ——

Please allow 2 to 4 weeks for delivery.
Prices subject to change without notice.

Enjoy More of Margaret Jensen's Delightful Bestsellers!

Quantity		Total
____	**LENA** — Inspirational true story of family reconciliation. The remarkable contribution of a college campus maid whose prayers, stories and songs uplifted students and staff alike. ISBN 0-89840-074-0/$7.99	$ ____
____	**VIOLETS FOR MR. B** — Meet patients, co-workers and doctors whom Margaret met over the years, share their suffering and triumphs, and marvel at the power of faith and dedication. ISBN 0-89840-211-5/$7.99	$ ____
____	**STORIES BY THE SEA** — True stories of the miraculous workings of God in the lives of '60s rebels who descended on the Jensen home after Ralph's conversion (see **Lena** for that story). ISBN 0-89840-288-3/$7.99	$ ____
____	**THE MARGARET JENSEN COLLECTION** — Four bestselling books in an attractive boxed set: **First We Have Coffee, Lena, Papa's Place** and **Violets for Mr. B.** An ideal gift — with a message — for anyone who loves a good story! ISBN 0-89840-231-X/$28.99	$ ____

Your Christian bookseller should have these products in stock. Please check with him before using this "Shop by Mail" Form.

Send completed order form to: **HERE'S LIFE PUBLISHERS, INC.**
P. O. Box 1576
San Bernardino, CA 92402-1576

Name _____

Address _____

State _____ Zip _____

☐ Payment enclosed
   (check or money order only)

☐ Visa   ☐ Mastercard

_____

Expiration Date _____

Signature _____

For faster service, call toll free:
1-800-950-4457

ORDER TOTAL $ ____

SHIPPING and HANDLING $ ____
($1.50 for one item, $0.50 for each additional. Do not exceed $4.00.)

APPLICABLE SALES TAX (CA 6.75%) $ ____

TOTAL DUE $ ____

Please allow 2 to 4 weeks for delivery.
Prices subject to change without notice.

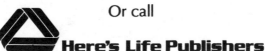